Assessment and Student Success in
a Differentiated Classroom

ASCD MEMBER BOOK

Many ASCD members received this book as a
member benefit upon its initial release.

Learn more at: **www.ascd.org/memberbooks**

Assessment and Student Success in a Differentiated Classroom

Carol Ann Tomlinson
Tonya R. Moon

Alexandria, Virginia USA

1703 N. Beauregard St. • Alexandria, VA 22311-1714 USA
Phone: 800-933-2723 or 703-578-9600 • Fax: 703-575-5400
Website: www.ascd.org • E-mail: member@ascd.org
Author guidelines: www.ascd.org/write

Gene R. Carter, *Executive Director*; Mary Catherine (MC) Desrosiers , *Chief Program Development Officer*; Richard Papale, *Publisher*; Genny Ostertag, *Acquisitions Editor*; Julie Houtz, *Director, Book Editing & Production*; Deborah Siegel, *Editor*; Georgia Park, *Senior Graphic Designer*; Mike Kalyan, *Production Manager*; Keith Demmons, *Desktop Publishing Specialist*; Kyle Steichen, *Production Specialist*

Printed in the United States of America. Cover art © 2013 by ASCD. ASCD publications present a variety of viewpoints. The views expressed or implied in this book should not be interpreted as official positions of the Association.

All web links in this book are correct as of the publication date below but may have become inactive or otherwise modified since that time. If you notice a deactivated or changed link, please e-mail books@ascd.org with the words "Link Update" in the subject line. In your message, please specify the web link, the book title, and the page number on which the link appears.

ASCD Member Book, No. FY14-1 (Sept. 2013, PSI+). ASCD Member Books mail to Premium (P), Select (S), and Institutional Plus (I+) members on this schedule: Jan., PSI+; Feb., P; Apr., PSI+; May, P; July, PSI+; Aug., P; Sept., PSI+; Nov., PSI+; Dec., P. Select membership was formerly known as Comprehensive membership.

PAPERBACK ISBN: 978-1-4166-1617-7   ASCD product #108028
Also available as an e-book (see Books in Print for the ISBNs).

Quantity discounts: 10–49 copies, 10%; 50+ copies, 15%; for 1,000 or more copies, call 800-933-2723, ext. 5634, or 703-575-5634. For desk copies: www.ascd.org/deskcopy

Library of Congress Cataloging-in-Publication Data
Tomlinson, Carol A.
 Assessment and student success in a differentiated classroom / Carol Ann Tomlinson and Tonya R. Moon.
   pages cm
 Includes bibliographical references and index.
 ISBN 978-1-4166-1617-7 (pbk. : alk. paper) 1. Individualized instruction—United States. 2. Educational tests and measurements. I. Title.
 LB1031.T64 2013
 371.39'4—dc23
                              2013021045

22 21 20 19 18 17 16 15 14 13   1 2 3 4 5 6 7 8 9 10 11 12

Assessment and Student Success in a Differentiated Classroom

Preface

When you starts measuring somebody, measure him right, child, measure him right. Make sure you done take into account what hills and valleys he come through before he got to wherever he is.

—Lorraine Hansberry, *A Raisin in the Sun*

As I suspect is the case for many teachers, my early teaching career was shaped more by my experiences as a K–12 and university student than by anything I learned in teacher education classes, and certainly more than by any clearly defined sense of what constitutes substantive teaching and learning. What I had seen my teachers do was, in large measure, what I did. I "played school" to learn how to teach in much the same way that children "play house" to learn how to become adults. And the gap between my role-playing and the art of teaching was about the same as the gap between playing house and artful parenting.

The chasm between how I thought about and planned for teaching and what I needed to do to lift my students' prospects significantly was most evident in my understanding (or lack of understanding) of assessment. In fact, I have no recollection of the presence of that word in my active educational lexicon. Had someone asked me to define *assessment*, I'd likely have responded, "Oh, sure. That means tests, grades, and report cards." Those three elements *were* clear in my thinking. I found grades and report cards to be aversive. Tests were something of a game, I suppose, up to a point.

My test-making strategy went something like this. At key junctures in a marking period, I realized I needed some grades, or that my students needed a dose of accountability, or that the unit I was teaching was nearing a point of conclusion—the end of a subtopic, the end of the unit, the midterm, or the end of a grading cycle. Then I sat down to create a test. I reflected on what my students and I had been exploring and tried to hit the high points. I worked to ensure that the test questions called on students to be thoughtful with the information and ideas rather than simply parroting them back (one point in my favor), and I often tried to include a couple of questions that students could answer only if they'd been paying close attention. I thought about the length of the test. My general idea was that a test should require students to work with focus for the entire class period—which meant they had to use their time judiciously to finish and few would "finish early." I wanted the students to succeed but also wanted them to understand that they'd have to invest in what we were studying in order to succeed. Although my thinking about measurement of student development was way off the mark, I didn't really mind test-making. It seemed a bit creative and did have a gamelike aspect to it—with the goal, I suppose, of stretching my students but not defeating them.

Giving and grading tests, however, were less satisfactory aspects of the whole assessment process. Some students got nervous and felt defeated at test time. Others made good grades on the tests but finished them too soon. (It was a good while before I identified that as an issue of low challenge for those students, and longer still before I understood that it was unlikely a single test could be at a challenge level appropriate for all of the students in my class.) Further, I never liked grading papers. It took a long time to read and make comments on them, and students didn't seem to spend much time reflecting on my feedback.

My dislike for assessment peaked during the four times a year when I had to "average grades," fill out report cards, ponder my students' responses to report cards, and talk with their parents. I was glad that process happened rapidly, if not painlessly.

I was most uncomfortable with what felt to me like a sense of betrayal of my students at report card time. In the first place, I worked hard to be open and honest with my students. Report cards felt secretive, and the message they bore often seemed surprising, if not shocking, to some students. Worse, though, was the disconnect between the report cards and the fact that I was faithful in conveying to students my trust in their capacity to learn and my own willingness to work hard to support that success. For many students, report cards seemed to be an incongruent moment of judgment that interrupted my usual message of confidence and partnership.

I recall with painful clarity a time in my third year of teaching when I stood in my classroom door as students entered our room on the morning after I'd completed report cards for the first marking period. The students didn't yet know what their grades would be, but I felt great discomfort in being aware of the disappointment some of them would experience when report cards were distributed at the end of the school day. I felt dishonest as I greeted those students with enthusiasm and affirmation. As one boy who had great difficulty with reading smiled at me and entered the room with optimism, I felt a keen sense of betrayal.

I had a lightning-bolt thought at that moment. I could fill out the report cards that night for the rest of the school year and would likely be about 95 percent accurate in doing so, even though we had not yet worked with the content that would be reflected in those report cards. There was something about report cards that reinforced the status quo rather than inviting human transformation. That jolting insight contributed significantly to my awareness that what I much later dubbed "differentiation" was an imperative if I was to succeed as a teacher and if my students were to succeed as learners. Sad to say, the epiphany did not cause me to rethink, discover, or invent a better approach to assessment for a long time.

Finally, there was the uncomfortable self-justification aspect of assessment that loomed at the end of the testing and grading process. I always welcomed input from parents (another point in my favor). I looked forward to the opportunity parent nights provided to understand my students better. Nonetheless, those events included an element of needing to justify myself—not so much my teaching, but at least my grading practices.

I went to parent nights armed with my gradebook and its rows of grades beside student names. I entered "big grades" (I had no idea those were summative assessments) in red and "little grades" (pop quizzes, journal entries, homework assignments) in black or blue. I was prepared to show parents the 12 or 15 or 17 grades beside their child's name, explain to them what topic each grade represented, and demonstrate how I averaged the string of grades to arrive at a report card grade. All of that projected a sense of precision, care, and competence I hoped indicated to parents that their child's grade was trustworthy.

At best, assessment was a periodic interruption in the flow of teaching and learning, and I resented it. It ran counter to what I wanted the classroom to be for my students and for me. I tolerated assessment because I had no choice. It was a necessary evil that came with the decision to teach.

Room for Growth

In my early years of teaching, the fabric of my understanding about assessment had so many flaws that it was best suited to making new clothes for the emperor. I simply didn't know what I was doing. My understanding about assessment and my resulting behaviors could be synthesized as follows:

- Assessment was mostly about grades and report cards.
- Assessment seemed an impediment to building student competence rather than a mechanism for doing so.
- Assessment was a threat to creating a safe, supportive learning environment rather than a means to that end.
- Assessment threatened to undermine my goal of strengthening students' efficacy rather than being a direct route to doing so.

- Assessment potentially created an adversarial teacher-student relationship and reduced students to a number or a letter or a percentage.
- Assessment devoured rather than created powerful learning moments.
- My teaching and learning goals were imprecise at best; students had to engage in mind-reading to understand their learning targets.
- Assessments were loosely linked with my ambiguous goals.
- I graded everything students did with no sense of their need for practice without judgment.
- I assumed grades motivated students to learn.
- Despite my distaste in doing so, I sometimes used grades as bribes or carrots or sticks.
- My feedback was too often in the category of "Nice job!" or "Good idea!" or "I like how you did this."
- Report card grades were a stew of academic performance, attitude, participation, citizenship, work habits, and goodness knows what else.
- I rarely engaged students in thinking about their assessment outcomes relative to learning goals.
- I seldom asked students to examine their learning practices or to set learning goals based on what assessment was showing us.
- Most regrettably, in those early years of teaching, I used assessments to grade and grades to fill the grade book.
- I simply did not see that the assessments were shouting at me to change my teaching practices to address students' learning needs.

My metamorphosis in coming to understand what effective use of assessment looked like and ultimately appreciating its great potential to enhance teaching and learning was glacially slow. While I devotedly worked to create a learning environment that energized my students, sought better models for thinking about curriculum, and invented instructional approaches that helped my students move forward, I continued to see assessment as an interloper in an otherwise positive (or at least evolving) landscape. For that reason—and because no one suggested I might want to reconsider my distaste for assessment—I continued to skirt it, push it to the margins of my pedagogical considerations. I suppose my unconscious conclusion was that if everything else was working well, the assessment piece wouldn't be a spoiler. Certainly I made noteworthy progress with integrating effective assessment routines into my thinking and my practice over the 20 years I spent in public school classrooms. That said, however, it remained the aspect of my work that I understood least and neglected most.

I periodically find myself thinking I want to go back to the classroom and redo the time I spent there so I can use an instructional strategy that seems promising to me, or apply a deeper understanding I have achieved about a particular learning issue, or study a perplexing issue. That desire to enter rewind mode is never more emphatic than when I consider how differently I'd think about assessment if I'd known then what I've learned since I left public school teaching. This book is an opportunity to share with classroom practitioners what I wish I'd known to do in the area of assessment.

Still Room for Growth

I believe the need to understand the power of effective assessment is still great in today's classrooms, with their broad and growing mix of students, all of whom need preparation for a complex and rapidly changing world. I believe the pressure to misuse assessment today is great as well. My early understanding of assessment was anemic, at least in part because the topic simply wasn't discussed in any significant way in conversations or in the scant professional development available at the time. Current teachers suffer not from inattention to assessment but rather from an overdose of what, in my estimation, is an unfortunate skewing of the topic. Assessment has now come to mean a standardized test or an end-of-course test. Teachers and students alike are judged—sometimes with tragically negative consequences—based on results of those circle-the-right-response tests. Other assessments are part of the conversation, of course. Those tend also to be packaged and standardized "benchmark" tests or interim assessments that are deemed important in ensuring that students will do well on the year-end assessments. And much of the current debate is on the degree to which report cards should or shouldn't mirror the degree to which students show mastery of the information measured by the assessments.

The era of common core standards is underway in the United States. Perhaps the fact that this iteration of standards advocates complex thinking so that students come to understand the disciplines and can use what they learn beyond the classroom and the year-end test bodes well for a better understanding of teaching and learning—including assessment. Nonetheless, certain enduring—and assessment-related—realities remain at the core of teaching and learning. Unless the educational frameworks we follow nurture a teacher's capacity to enact these truths in daily practice, our schools, our profession, and our students will come up short. Among the most important of these truths are the following:

- Teaching is about perpetuating the human desire to understand the world around us so the young people we teach become increasingly engaged and informed stewards of that world.
- Learning happens when students care about what they are studying and feel safe and supported in taking the risk of learning.

- People learn more readily, more efficiently, when what they attempt to learn connects with their lives and experiences and when it leads them to understanding.
- Learning happens *within* people, not *to* them; because of that, learning is a messy process and cannot always happen on a prescribed time line or in the same way for all individuals.
- A key aspect of learning is an individual's belief in his or her capacity to learn.
- Successful learners understand the learning process, accept it as worthy of time and effort, and accept the centrality of their role in contributing to their success.
- How teachers view learners and learning shapes how young people see themselves as human beings and as learners.
- Every aspect or element of the classroom is related to every other one. Learning environment, curriculum, assessment, instruction, and classroom leadership and management are absolutely interdependent. When one of the elements is strengthened, all of them benefit; when one is diluted, all are diminished.

Teaching with these truths or principles at the center of thinking about, planning for, and implementing classroom practice is a tall order. But it is a goal well worth pursuing when one considers that teaching is a profession that deals with young lives.

Considering classroom assessment in terms of the principles is a paradigm shift for many of us. It certainly was for me. It causes teachers to ask questions like these:

- How can assessment fuel rather than abate young people's curiosity about and interest in the discipline I teach?
- How can assessment sharpen my clarity about what matters most in the discipline, subject, and topics we explore?
- What are the characteristics of assessment that contribute to students' understanding and application of what they learn?
- How can assessment contribute to my belief that each of my students has the capacity to learn what matters most in the discipline or disciplines I teach?
- What is the nature of assessment that is a positive force in helping students to believe in their capacity to learn and to invest in using that capacity?
- How can assessment help the students I teach captain their success as learners in the classroom and beyond?
- In what ways might assessment contribute to my understanding of the similarities and differences my students bring to class—to knowing each of them as an individual?

- What is the potential of assessment information to help me teach in ways that reach more students more effectively?

Those are substantial questions. They exist in a different realm than my early sense that assessment was something my students and I had to endure. I wish I had known to ask the questions sooner in my work.

Looking Ahead

This book is a practical one designed for teachers who work in real classrooms, with real students, amid the real pressures of schools every day. My coauthor, Tonya Moon, and I hope it will provide a clear and useful framework for thinking about assessment and its role in student (and teacher) success. In this way, the book is a "how-to" book. We also hope, however, that it will help educators who study its ideas answer the essential questions that lead us to sustained growth and meaning-rich professional practice. Thus we aim also to create a "why" book. We believe that education, like all professions, is best served when practitioners draw from both the art and the science that undergird the work we do.

The chapters ahead first examine essential elements of differentiation, locating assessment in a structure that promotes awareness of the interdependence of the classroom elements—including the teacher and each student. Subsequent chapters look at pre-assessment; formative, or ongoing, assessment; summative assessment; and grading and reporting grades.

The ideas in the book are both better grounded and more robust because of the coauthorship of my University of Virginia colleague and friend, Tonya Moon. Measurement and assessment are her areas of expertise. She has been one of my teachers and mentors in these domains. We have worked together for many years on research, presentations, and teaching related to differentiated instruction. Her many contributions in authoring this book bring depth, rigor, and credibility to the topic of differentiation and assessment. I'm grateful for her partnership in this work, as I often am in the work we do jointly at the university.

—Carol Tomlinson

1

Differentiation: An Overview

Note that differentiation relates more to addressing students' different phases of learning from novice to capable to proficient rather than merely providing different activities to different (groups of) students.

—John Hattie, *Visible Learning for Teachers*

Differentiation of instruction is often misconstrued. It would be handy to represent differentiation as simply instructional decision making through which a teacher creates varied learning options to address students' diverse readiness levels, interests, and learning preferences. Although that approach is attractive because it simplifies teacher thinking, administrator feedback, and professional development design, it is ineffective and potentially dangerous. To see differentiation as an isolated element reduces teaching to a series of disconnected components that function effectively apart from the whole. The more difficult and elegant truth is that effective teaching is a system composed of interdependent elements. As with all systems, each part is enhanced when others are enhanced, and each part is diminished when any part is weakened.

Robust teaching links five classroom elements so that each one flows from, feeds, and enhances the others. Those elements are learning environment, curriculum, assessment, instruction, and classroom leadership and management (Tomlinson & Moon, 2013). This chapter provides a brief overview of each of the elements as they relate to one another and to differentiation. Understanding the mutuality that excellent teachers strive to achieve among the elements also establishes a clear context for an extended discussion of the powerful role of assessment in differentiation. Figure 1.1 provides a flowchart or concept map of the key elements of differentiation.

Figure 1.1
Key Elements of Effective Differentiated Instruction

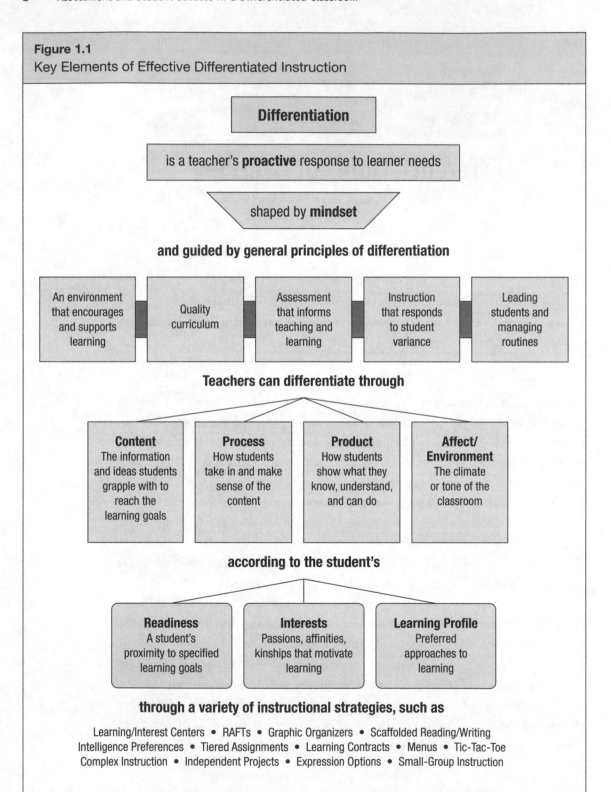

Learning Environment and Differentiation

Learning environment refers to both the physical and the affective climate in the classroom. It is the "weather" that affects everything that happens there. Few students enter a classroom at the outset of a new school year asking, "What can you teach me about grammar?" (or the periodic table or cursive writing or planets). Rather, they come with an overriding question: "How is it going to be for me in this place?" The nature of the learning environment for that young person will, in large measure, answer that question.

Regardless of the age of the learners, they ask questions such as these (Tomlinson, 2003):

- Will I be affirmed in this place? (Will people accept me here—find me acceptable? Will I be safe here as I am? Will people listen to me and hear me? Will someone know how I'm doing and how I'm feeling? Will they care? Will people value my interests and dreams? Will my perspectives be honored and acted upon? Will people here believe in me and in my capacity to succeed?)
- Can I make a contribution in this place? (Will I make a positive difference in the work that goes on here? Do I bring unique and important abilities to the work we need to do? Can I help others and the class as a whole do better work and accomplish more important things than if I weren't here? Will I feel connected to others through common goals?)
- Will I grow in power here? (Is what I learn going to be useful to me now as well as later? Will I learn to make choices that contribute to my success? Will I understand how this place operates and what is expected of me here? Will I know what quality looks like and how to achieve it? Is there dependable support here for my journey?)
- Do I see purpose in what we do here? (Do I understand what I'm asked to learn? Will I see meaning and significance in what we do? Will what we learn reflect me and my world? Will the work engage and absorb me?)
- Will I be stretched and challenged in this place? (Will the work complement my abilities? Will it call on me to work hard and to work smart? Will I be increasingly accountable for my own growth and contribution to the growth of others? Will I regularly achieve here things I initially think are out of my reach?)

Many years ago, Hiam Ginott (1972) argued that the teacher is the weather-maker in the classroom, with the teacher's response to every classroom situation being the determining factor in whether a child is inspired or tortured, humanized or dehumanized, hurt or healed. In fact, research has repeatedly indicated that a teacher's emotional connection with a student is a potent contributor to academic growth (Allen, Gregory,

Mikami, Hamre, & Pianta, 2012; Hattie, 2009). That connection enables the student to trust that the teacher is a dependable partner in achievement.

In a differentiated classroom, the teacher's aim is to make the classroom work for each student who is obliged to spend time there. Thus the teacher is attuned to the students' various needs and responds to ensure that the needs are met. Various scholars (Berger, 2003; Dweck, 2008; Hattie, 2012b; Tomlinson, 2003) have noted that the teacher's response to student needs includes the following:

- Belief—Confidence in the students' capacity to succeed through hard work and support—what Dweck (2008) calls a "growth mindset"; the conviction that it is the students' committed work rather than heredity or home environment that will have the greatest impact on their success.
- Invitation—Respect for the students, who they are, and who they might become; a desire to know the students well in order to teach them well; awareness of what makes each student unique, including strengths and weaknesses; time to talk with and listen to the students; a message that the classroom belongs to the students, too; evidence that the students are needed for the classroom to be as effective as it should be.
- Investment—Working hard to make the classroom work for the students and to reflect the strengths of the students in it; enjoyment in thinking about the classroom, the students, and the shared work; satisfaction in finding new ways to help students grow; determination to do whatever it takes to ensure the growth of each student.
- Opportunity—Important, worthy, and daunting things for the students to do; a sense of new possibilities; a sense of partnership; roles that contribute to the success of the class and to the growth of the students; expectation of and coaching for quality work.
- Persistence—An ethic of continual growth; no finish line in learning for teacher or students; no excuses; figuring out what works best to support success; the message that there's always another way to approach learning.
- Reflection—Watching and listening to students carefully; using observations and information to make sure each student has consistent opportunity to learn and succeed; working to see the world through the student's eyes; asking what's working and what can work better.

The teacher has the opportunity to issue an irresistible invitation to learn. Such an invitation has three hallmarks: (1) unerring respect for each student's value, ability, and responsibility; (2) unflagging optimism that every student has the untapped capacity to learn what is being taught; and (3) active and visible support for student success (Hattie,

2012b; Skinner, Furrer, Marchand, & Kindermann, 2008). When a teacher exhibits these hallmarks, students feel the teacher is trustworthy—will be a reliable partner in the difficult and risky work of real learning. That feeling enables the teacher to forge connections with students as individuals.

These teacher-student connections provide opportunity for a teacher to know students in a more realistic and multidimensional way than would be the case without such mutual trust. They create a foundation for addressing issues and problems in a positive and productive way. They attend to the human need to know and be known. Teacher-student connections also pave the way for the teacher to build a collection of disparate individuals into a team with a common cause—maximum academic growth for each member of the group. In such classrooms, students work together and display the characteristics of an effective team. They learn how to collaborate. They use their complementary skills to enable each member to capitalize on strengths and minimize weaknesses. They learn responsibility for themselves, for one another, and for class processes and routines.

The way in which students experience the classroom learning environment profoundly shapes how they experience learning. Nonetheless, the other classroom elements also profoundly affect the nature of the learning environment. For example, if the curriculum is flat, uninspired, or seems to be out of reach or detached from a student's world, that student's need for challenge, purpose, and power goes unmet and the learning environment suffers. If assessment feels punitive and fails to provide a student with information about how to succeed with important goals, the environment feels uncertain because challenge and support are out of balance. If instruction is not responsive to student needs in terms of readiness, interest, and approach to learning, the environment does not feel safe and the student does not feel known, valued, appreciated, or heard. Finally, if classroom leadership and management suggests a lack of trust in students and is either rigid or ill structured, the learning process is impaired and, once again, the environment is marred. Every element in the classroom system touches every other element in ways that build up or diminish those elements and classroom effectiveness as a whole.

Curriculum and Differentiation

One way of envisioning curriculum is to think of it as what teachers plan to teach—and what they want students to learn. The more difficult question involves delineating the characteristics of *quality* curriculum—in other words, the nature of what we should teach and what we should ask our students to learn. Although that question has no single answer, ample evidence (e.g., National Research Council, 2000; Sousa & Tomlinson, 2011; Tomlinson & McTighe, 2006; Wiggins & McTighe, 1998) suggests that curriculum should, at the very least, have three fundamental attributes. First, it should have *clear goals* for what students should know, understand, and be able to do as the result of any segment of learning. Second, it should result in *student understanding* of important content (versus largely rote memory of content). Third, it should *engage students* in the process of learning.

Goal Clarity

Although nearly all teachers can report what they will "cover" in a lesson or unit and what their students will do in the lesson or unit, few can specify precisely what students should know, understand, and be able to do as a result of participating in those segments of learning. Without precision in what we've called KUDs (what we want students to *k*now, *u*nderstand, and be able to *d*o), several predictable and costly problems arise. Because learning destinations are ambiguous, instruction drifts. In addition, students are unclear about what really matters in content and spend a great deal of time trying to figure out what teachers will ask on a test rather than focusing on how ideas work and how to use them. Third, assessment and instruction lack symmetry or congruence. What teachers talk about in class, what students do, and how they are asked to demonstrate what they've learned likely have some overlap, but not a hand-in-glove match.

From the standpoint of differentiation, lack of clarity about KUDs makes it difficult, if not impossible, to differentiate effectively. A common approach occurs when teachers "differentiate" by assigning less work to students who struggle with content and more work to students who grasp it readily. But it is neither useful to do less of what you don't understand nor more of what you already know. Effective differentiation is most likely to occur when a teacher is (1) clear about a student's status with specified KUDs, (2) able to plan to move students forward with knowledge and skill once they have mastered required sequences, and (3) able to "teach backward" to help students who lack essential knowledge and skill achieve mastery, even while moving the class ahead. In differentiating understandings, teachers are likely to be most effective when they have all students work with the same essential understandings but at varied levels of complexity and with different scaffolding based on the students' current points of development. These more defensible approaches to differentiation are unavailable, however, without clear KUDs.

Focus on Understanding

If we intend for students to be able to use what they "learn," memorization is an unreliable method to accomplish that goal. Students fail to remember much of what they try to drill into their brains by rote recall, even in the short term. Further, they can't apply, transfer, or create with "knowledge" they don't understand—even if they do recall it (National Research Council, 2000; Sousa & Tomlinson, 2011; Wiggins & McTighe, 1998). Understanding requires students to learn, make sense of, and use content. It also suggests that the *U* in *KUD* is pivotal. Making understanding central in curriculum calls on teachers themselves to be aware of what makes their content powerful in the lives of people who work with it, how the content is organized to make meaning, and how it can connect with the lives and experiences of their students. It also calls on a teacher to create sense-making tasks for students in which they use important knowledge and skills to explore, apply, extend, and create with essential understandings.

In terms of differentiation, creating understanding-focused curriculum asks teachers to realize that students will approach understanding at varied levels of sophistication, will need different support systems to increase their current level of understanding of any principle, and will need a range of analogies or applications to connect the understanding with their own life experiences. In terms of assessment, an understanding-focused curriculum suggests that pre-assessments, formative (ongoing) assessments, and summative assessments will center on student understanding at least as vigorously—and generally more so—than on knowledge and skill. In fact, assessments that help students connect knowledge, understanding, and skill will be particularly potent in the learning process.

Engagement

There is a clear link, of course, between understanding and engagement. It's difficult to invest over time in content and ideas that feel inaccessible or estranged from personal experience. Engagement in the classroom results when a student's attention is attracted to an idea or a task and is held there because the idea or task seems worthwhile. Students become engrossed because the task is enjoyable, or because it seems to provide them with the power of competence or autonomy, or because it links with an experience, interest, or talent that is significant to them, or because it is at the right level of challenge to stimulate rather than frustrate or bore them—or likely because of a combination of these conditions. When students are engaged, they are more likely to concentrate, remain absorbed with a task, persist in the face of difficulty, experience satisfaction, and feel pride in what they do. Conversely, lack of engagement leads to inattention, giving up, withdrawal, boredom, and frustration, anger, or self-blame (Skinner et al., 2008). Curriculum that promotes understanding is engaging in a way that drill and rote memory seldom are, and conversely, curriculum that is engaging causes students to persist in achieving understanding. Phil Schlechty (1997) says that the first job of schools (and the second and the third . . .) is to produce curriculum that is so engaging for students that they keep working even when the going gets tough, and that results in a sense of satisfaction and even delight when they accomplish what the work asks of them.

In terms of differentiation, tasks will sometimes need to be at different degrees of difficulty or linked to different experiences, interests, and talents in order to engage a broad range of learners. In terms of assessment, it's useful to realize that students are less likely to invest effort in assessments that they see as detached from their lives and experiences, or that are at a level of challenge that is out of sync with their current point of development.

"Teaching Up"

In addition to goal clarity, a focus on understanding, and the ability to engage students, quality curriculum has one additional characteristic that aligns with a sound philosophy of differentiation: the principle of "teaching up." When designing a differentiated task to address student readiness needs, a teacher must decide on a starting point for planning. Is it best to plan first for the "typical," or "grade-level," student and then differentiate by making some tasks easier? Or perhaps it makes better sense to begin with designing work for students who struggle with particular content and then to enrich the work for students whose proficiency is beyond basic. In fact, a third option is far more powerful on several levels. If teachers routinely began planning student work by developing tasks that would invigorate students who are advanced in a topic or content area and then differentiate by providing scaffolding that enables the range of less advanced learners to work successfully with the advanced-level task, achievement would be accelerated for many other students. Further, "teaching up" has at its core a connection between curriculum and learning environment. When teachers believe unequivocally in the capacity of their students to succeed through hard work and perseverance, it's natural to provide work that complements the capacity of each student to think, problem solve, and make meaning of important ideas. "Teaching up" communicates clearly that everyone in the class is worthy of the best curriculum the teacher knows how to create. Differentiation makes it possible for a broad range of students to step up to the challenge.

Assessment and Differentiation

If teachers strongly believe in the ability of their content and curriculum to improve students' prospects and lives and in the worth and potential of their students, it follows that they would be eager to know how each student is progressing toward achieving important learning goals—and going beyond. Teachers would no more want any of their students to persist in feeling frustrated and anxious or to languish in boredom than they would want that to happen to their own child. Assessment would be as natural a diagnostic process in the classroom as it is in a good medical context. The teacher simply must have a regular and evolving sense of a student's academic progress to plan for that student's academic health. For differentiation to be effective, teachers need to know, for each student, where that student begins and where that student is in the individual journey toward meeting the criteria of the lesson or unit (Hattie, 2012b). In other words, assessment is the compass for daily planning in a differentiated classroom.

The remaining chapters in this book explore how assessment guides instruction that is designed to work for a variety of learners. Chapter 2 establishes a foundation for thinking about assessment and differentiation.

Instruction and Differentiation

Whereas curriculum refers to *what* teachers teach or *what* students should learn, instruction refers to *how* teachers teach or *how* students will experience learning. A number of researchers argue that instruction is more powerful in student learning than is curriculum. Dylan Wiliam (2011) notes, "A bad curriculum well taught is invariably a better experience for students than a good curriculum badly taught: pedagogy trumps curriculum. Or more precisely, pedagogy *is* curriculum, because what matters is how things are taught, rather than what is taught" (p. 13). John Hattie (2009) reflects, "It is less the content of curricula that is important than the strategies teachers use to implement the curriculum so students progress upwards through the curricula content" (p. 159). Max van Manen (1991) reminds us that the most important pedagogical question a teacher can ask is how a particular learner is experiencing what's being taught.

Indeed, instruction is at the core of differentiation because the ultimate goal of differentiation is to ensure that each student has the best possible learning experiences in order to maximize academic growth. (We are not referring to growth defined by standardized test scores, but rather by a variety of indicators of development in knowledge, understanding, skill, engagement with learning, and autonomy as a learner.) Achieving the goal of maximum academic growth, however, is dependent upon effective instructional practices working in concert with an effective curriculum, as well as effective assessment, and classroom leadership and management. In other words, instruction that is effective in moving students ahead from their starting points will (1) benefit from and contribute to a positive learning community, (2) be targeted at helping students acquire and use the specified learning targets (KUDs), (3) be informed by pre-assessment and formative (ongoing) assessment, and (4) necessitate flexible classroom routines and student participation in those routines in a way that accommodates students' varying needs.

Sometimes teacher observation, the goals of the day, and assessment information will indicate that the whole class might benefit from the same instruction. In those cases, of course, differentiation isn't necessary. On the other hand, there will be many times when some students are ahead of or behind others in a particular segment of learning, or when students would benefit from connecting learning targets (KUDs) with their particular interests, or when it's sensible to offer students more than one path to accomplish important goals. In those instances, students are well served when teachers address their particular needs as well as the needs of the class as a whole—in other words, when teachers differentiate instruction based on students' readiness, their interests, and their preferred approaches to learning.

Readiness

Readiness is not a synonym for ability or capacity to learn. Rather, it refers to a student's proximity to specified learning goals. A student's actual ability is much like an iceberg. Only a small portion of it is visible; much more lies beyond our view. Nonetheless, we often err by classifying students according to what we perceive to be their ability and teaching them accordingly. That's most often a grievous error. Planning instruction based on what we think is a student's capacity to learn leads us to ask, "What *can* this student do?" Planning instruction based on readiness guides us to ask, "What does this student *need* to do in order to succeed?" The term *readiness* aligns with a growth mind-set—both flowing from and feeding it. Many instructional approaches enable teachers to attend to a range of readiness needs. These approaches include, but certainly are not limited to, the following: tiering, small-group instruction, use of reading materials at varied levels of readability, learning contracts, learning centers, compacting, flexible time spans for work, personalized goals, and use of technology to assist students with reading, writing, or other learning needs.

Interest

Interest is a great motivator for learning. Interest can refer to a topic or skill that taps into a student's talents or experiences or dreams—an area of current passion for the student. It can also refer simply to ideas, skills, or work that is appealing to a student. The term might also be used to think about new possibilities a student could encounter in the classroom that would be a source of future passions. In any case, students invest more in or become more engaged with that which interests them.

An artful teacher helps students see themselves, their lives, their talents, and their aspirations in the curriculum they study. That happens, for example, when a high school history teacher invites students to learn about contributors from many cultures to an event or a time period; when a middle school math teacher supports students in studying the mathematics of music or the science of art; when an elementary music teacher helps students see that music is self-expression; or when a world language teacher guides students in comparing the language of their neighborhood to the language they are studying in class. It happens when a high school teacher shows students the mathematics involved in 3-D structures and angles in skateboard parks so that math is not reduced to a series of operations and algorithms. Students also see their interests in school subjects when a middle school English teacher gives a student "permission" to study theories of dinosaur extinction for an English assignment, even though the focus of the work is science; or when a high school history teacher invites a student talented in art to draw caricatures of key historical figures for display and discussion in the classroom; or when a technology teacher asks students to build the prototype of a machine that can help to solve a problem they care about. Among instructional approaches that help students connect required content with their interests are independent studies, interest centers, anchor activities, the RAFT writing strategy, expert groups, Jigsaws, and authentic assessments.

Learning Profile

Nearly all people—teachers and students included—have stories about times when learning worked very well for them and times when it was awkward, painful, or hopeless. Learning-profile differentiation seeks to provide learners with approaches to learning that make the process both more efficient and more effective for them. Learning profiles, learning preferences, or preferred approaches to learning are shaped by gender, culture, the environment, biology, and a particular learning context. It is *not* the case that individuals have just one or two approaches to learning that are a match for them. It is *not* the case that a person learns best the same way in two different content areas or in two different topics within the same content area. For example, a student who learns the multiplication tables best by saying them orally may learn about latitude and longitude best by drawing or examining maps. Current research (Coffield, Moseley, Hall, & Ecclestone, 2004; Lisle, 2006; Pashler, McDaniel, Rohrer, & Bjork, 2008) and wisdom generally do *not* support using surveys or questionnaires or other assessments to "determine" a student's learning style or intelligence preference, and certainly do *not* support assigning a student a particular learning-style or intelligence-preference label, or assigning tasks based on assumptions about learning style. Rather, the goal of learning-profile differentiation should be to create more ways for students to take in, engage with, explore, and demonstrate knowledge about content, and then to help students develop awareness of which approaches to learning work best for them under which circumstances, and to guide them to know when to change approaches for better learning outcomes (Tomlinson & Imbeau, 2013). Teachers and students need to understand that categorizing or pigeonholing people is to both misjudge and limit them. Some of the strategies useful in providing students with approaches to learning that will work for them in a particular context include the following: RAFTs, learning contracts or menus, Tri-Mind, synthesis groups, different work-group options (such as work alone, with a partner, or with a small group), and varied expression options and tools for class assignments, homework, and assessments.

Flexible Grouping and Respectful Tasks

Two key principles of effective differentiation related to instruction are flexible grouping and respectful tasks. Flexible grouping stresses the importance of proactive instructional planning to ensure that students regularly and frequently have the opportunity to work with a wide variety of peers. Within a short time, students should work with peers who have readiness needs similar to their own and peers with a variety of readiness points; peers who share their particular interests and peers who have interests quite different from their own; peers who want to approach a learning task as the student does and peers who approach learning differently; randomly grouped peers and peer groupings created by both teacher and student choice. Designed appropriately, these opportunities to work with many age-mates are important in broadening students' awareness and appreciation of their own strengths and needs and the strengths and needs of others. Flexible grouping also keeps students from perceiving themselves and others as "bluebirds, buzzards, and sparrows," while it helps teachers "audition" their students in a variety of learning contexts.

The principle of respectful tasks is also central to the success of differentiation. This directs us to ensure that each student's work is as interesting and inviting as every other student's work. It reminds teachers that every student should regularly encounter tasks that reflect the teacher's belief that the student is worthy and capable of grappling with and applying important ideas and skills—that the student is a critical thinker who can bring her skills to bear on addressing difficult issues and solving complex problems.

Components of Instructional Differentiation

Five components of instruction can be differentiated: (1) *content*—what a student needs to learn or how the student will gain access to the knowledge, ideas, and skills; (2) *process*—how the student will come to master and "own" the knowledge, ideas, and skills; (3) *product*—how the student will *summatively* show what he has learned; (4) *affect*—the climate that encompasses the learning and interactions among students and teacher; and (5) *learning environment*— the personal, social, and physical arrangements in the classroom. All of these elements can be differentiated to address students' readiness needs, their interests, and their learning profiles or preferences. Figure 1.2 provides an example of each of the five components modified to address each of the three areas of student variance.

Figure 1.2

Examples of Differentiation for Variations in Readiness, Interest, and Learning Profile

Components of Differentiation	Readiness	Interest	Learning Profile
Content	An elementary teacher uses digital video images of geological phenomena to support understanding of students who have no experience with the phenomena and who need to develop academic vocabulary related to the phenomena.	A biology teacher uses athletic teams, families, and rock bands to illustrate the concept of symbiosis.	During a poetry unit, a teacher finds more students are engaged when she discusses the creative aspects of poems and how the poems connect to students' lives (practical aspects) along with analytical aspects.
Process	Based on pre-assessment information, a primary teacher begins a unit on telling time by having some students work with telling time by the hour and half hour, some by telling time to five-minute intervals, and some by telling time to the minute.	Students look for examples of symmetry in objects they use at home or in hobbies and create an exhibit of their objects with an explanation of how they use the objects and why the objects represent symmetry.	Primary students must learn how Earth's rotation and revolution create day and night and season. To begin the unit, the teacher illustrates the concept of rotation by having students stand and rotate, find and explain objects that rotate, sing about rotation, and draw something that rotates.
Product	A middle school teacher provides all students with models of effective student products from prior years to help them analyze what quality work looks like. Although all of the examples demonstrate proficiency with KUDs, students who are more advanced with the content examine models at a higher degree of sophistication.	High school students studying Robert Frost's "Road Not Taken" use the life of a famous person or well-known character from movies or literature to demonstrate parallels between the events in the poem and in the life of the person they chose.	Elementary students use meteorological data to make a forecast for the week ahead in their town. All students must predict the weather and explain their prediction. They may write and illustrate the forecast for the local paper, present the forecast for TV, or create a weather map that depicts their forecast.
Affect	An algebra teacher watches students for signs of frustration as she explains complex concepts, and she stops for peer debriefing followed by Q&A when she thinks students feel they are getting lost.	A secondary teacher realizes several students in her classes resist challenging tasks. Early in the year, she makes sure to stress that evidence of persistence, seeking help, and revision are important, and she both encourages and acknowledges student contributions of effort to their success.	Sammy has great difficulty sitting still for more than a few minutes at a time and gets tense and inattentive as a result. The teacher has assigned him two seats on opposite sides of the room and has worked with him on when and how he can go from one seat to the other to move during whole-class lessons.
Environment	A middle school social studies teacher has created four room arrangements and posted four corresponding seating diagrams on a bulletin board to allow flexibility in presentation and interaction. Students all know which furniture to move and how to move it to go quickly from one configuration to another.	An elementary teacher has posted "help cards" in several places in the room so when students are working independently, they can easily find reminders about things such as how to save work to a folder on the computer, the elements of haiku, or rules for basic punctuation.	A classroom has portable carrels that students can place on their desks if movement of other students distracts them while they are working. There are also headphones and earplugs students can use if they are easily distracted by small-group conversations when they are working alone.

Instruction in a differentiated classroom is, not surprisingly, tightly interconnected with the other four classroom elements (curriculum, assessment, learning environment, and classroom leadership/management). It should be guided by the curriculum's KUDs and shaped by pre- and formative assessment. When instruction is a good fit for the variety of learners in the classroom, it influences the environment in a positive way, making it a safe place for the risk of learning. When instruction is ineffective for some or many students in a classroom, the environment becomes negative and deflects student attention away from learning and toward self-protection (Sousa & Tomlinson, 2011). Responsive instruction also contributes to community as students learn to appreciate the growth exhibited by their peers and the effort that fuels the growth. The component of classroom leadership and management, as we'll see in the next section, helps students understand the need for differentiation, contribute to its philosophy, participate actively in the success of its routines, and support one another and the teacher in making the classroom work for everyone who invests time there.

Classroom Leadership/Management and Differentiation

It goes without saying that when 20 or 30 or 40 young people gather in a limited space, the opportunity for some degree of bedlam is quite real. It also goes without saying that classrooms are not good places for *any* degree of bedlam. Not only can students not learn in that context, but a teacher can't maintain sanity, either. The bedrock questions asked by novice teachers, then, typically cluster around how to "manage" students. Even many veteran teachers never quite lose the niggling fear that they could lose control of the classroom in an instant.

As teachers, we often think of *classroom management* as a synonym for *control*. That approach, of course, positions a teacher in an adversarial role with young people whose nature is to move about (sometimes clumsily) and to speak at inopportune moments (sometimes too loudly). There is something in the makeup of human beings—teachers included—that resists being "managed."

A better way to think about creating a classroom in which teaching and learning can proceed predictably and productively is to see this aspect of the teacher's job as two-fold—leading students, and managing processes and routines (Tomlinson & Imbeau, 2013). Although we humans resist being managed, we are amenable to becoming part of an endeavor that we perceive to be meaningful and beneficial.

Leading in a differentiated classroom suggests that a teacher has a vision of a class-room where the welfare of each student is paramount, where members come together as a team to achieve important goals—a community designed to support the maximum development of each individual and the group as a whole. When a teacher can articulate that vision to students of any age, help them co-construct parameters by which such a community would operate, and systematically work with them to implement the vision, students understand and own the game plan in the classroom. "Let's work together to create a place where learning works for all of us" is a far more compelling invitation for most learners than "Please sit still and participate only upon invitation."

Such a visionary approach doesn't ensure that all students will function with maturity and equanimity all of the time, of course. What it does provide is a respectful, optimistic, growth mind-set–oriented way for a teacher to work with students to create an environment that balances structure and flexibility to accommodate all kinds of learners.

Managing routines and processes in differentiated classrooms suggests that the teacher will help students understand, contribute to, and participate in structures designed to facilitate learning. Some of the routines and processes help the teacher work efficiently and effectively; others help students work efficiently and effectively. Most involve collaborative work between the teacher and the students. The processes necessary for "flexible order" in the classroom include the following:

- Arranging the classroom so materials that students need are easily accessible
- Giving directions for tasks in which not all students will do the same work
- Keeping conversational noise at a reasonable level when students work together
- Providing ways for students to get help when the teacher is working with individuals or small groups
- Providing guidelines for what a student should do (and how) when an assigned task is completed
- Sharing expectations for moving around the classroom
- Ensuring that students know how and when to help peers who need assistance
- Ensuring that students know where to put completed work
- Having expectations for keeping materials and supplies in order

Flexible classroom management not only is essential for differentiation, but also is an imperative for a classroom in which students are expected to engage with intellectually challenging ideas and to be thinkers, problem-solvers, and collaborators (LePage, Darling-Hammond, & Akar, 2005). Thus curriculum focused on engagement and understanding as well as "teaching up" requires a flexible approach to teaching and learning. This approach also creates an environment that provides affirmation, challenge, and support to a full range of learners, creating a safe place for those students to learn. It exemplifies the growth mindset of teachers who believe in the capacity of their students not only to learn what's necessary for success, but also to work responsibly to support that success. Further, formative assessment is of little use if rigid classroom management curbs a teacher's willingness to provide learning options that assessment data indicate are necessary so that students can take their particular next steps forward in learning.

In translating for teachers his findings from over 800 meta-analyses of research on student achievement, John Hattie (2012b) reflects on key conclusions of the landmark book *How People Learn* (National Research Council, 2000) and concludes that effective classrooms will have four defining characteristics:

1. Student centered—because teaching is all about where a student is on the journey from novice to competent to proficient.

2. Knowledge-centered—because there must be clear and important knowledge so students can make connections and relationships among ideas.

3. Assessment-rich—to better understand where students are throughout the journey in order for the teacher and students to know where to go next, so that each student can move ahead from his or her starting point.

4. Community-centered—because there is no one way from novice to proficient, teachers and students need to share and learn from one another, share the trials, tribulations, and triumphs of how each person progresses, and share the relevance of what the community's members are aiming to learn.

These are also attributes of effectively differentiated classrooms in which learning environment, curriculum, assessment, instruction, and classroom leadership and management work in concert with the goal of helping each learner progress as far as possible with powerful learning goals. In the remainder of the book, we focus on one of these interconnected elements—assessment. It's important to recall, however, that the elements must work together in ways that both research and practice reveal are beneficial to students' learning and their development as learners.

❧ ❧ ❧ ❧ ❧

The focus of this book is differentiation and assessment. If you would like to read more about differentiation as a whole and about the role of the various elements as discussed in this chapter, see the suggested books in the appendix.

2

Assessment and Differentiation: A Framework for Understanding

From a pedagogical perspective, the most important question is always, "How did the young person experience this particular situation, relationship, or event?"

—Max van Manen, *The Tact of Teaching*

For competent physicians, diagnosis is a foundational element of practice. Certainly it is helpful when doctors connect with patients in a way that builds trust, opens lines of honest communication, and motivates patients to follow their advice. Clearly it is essential that doctors have a solid and evolving knowledge of the science behind their areas of practice. These days, doctors also benefit from business acumen and must stay abreast of insurance regulations, associated laws, and rapidly changing pharmaceuticals. Still, diagnosis is fundamental to linking the patient's current needs to the best possible options and outcomes for that patient. It is a rare event when doctors prescribe without diagnosing.

Teachers, too, need to connect with students to build trust, to open lines of communication, and to motivate students to follow their advice. Teachers, like doctors, need solid and evolving knowledge of the content and science of their discipline. And, like medicine, teaching is a multidimensional profession that calls on teachers to be arbiters, salespersons, lawyers, counselors, and negotiators—to name a few associated roles. Nonetheless, assessment in an effectively differentiated classroom is the foundation of successful instructional planning. It is the teacher's analog to the doctor's use of diagnosis. It is the process of coming to understand a student's current learning needs well enough to plan for the best possible instructional processes and outcomes for each learner whose academic welfare is the teacher's responsibility. Unfortunately, teachers often do prescribe without a diagnosis.

The goal of this chapter is to provide a framework for thinking about assessment in the chapters that follow, and more to the point, for thinking about assessment as an invaluable element in classroom practice. We'll take an initial look at kinds of assessment; the when, what, and why of assessment; a line of logic, or game plan, for assessment; and how assessment affects the other classroom elements (learning environment, curriculum, instruction, and leadership and management). Then we'll revisit these topics in later chapters, with a more specific focus.

Kinds of Assessments

Classroom assessment is the process of collecting, synthesizing, and interpreting information in a classroom for the purpose of aiding a teacher's decision making. It includes a broad range of information that helps teachers understand their students, monitor teaching and learning, and build an effective classroom community. Teachers use assessment to do the following: diagnose student problems, make judgments about student academic performance, form student work groups, develop instructional plans, and effectively lead and manage a classroom (Airasian, 1997). The emphasis in this book, and in a differentiated classroom, is on assessment to inform instruction. The term *assessment* derives from the Latin *assidere*, meaning "to sit beside" (Wiggins, 1993).

There are essentially two kinds of classroom assessments: formative and summative. Formative assessment is sometimes called *ongoing* assessment. It is a process used to guide, mentor, direct, and encourage student growth. Teachers use ongoing or formative assessment to consistently monitor students' developing knowledge, understanding, and skill related to the topic at hand in order to know how to proceed with instruction in a way that maximizes the opportunity for student growth and success with key content. An assessment can be considered formative if a teacher gathers evidence about student performance, interprets the evidence, and uses the evidence to make decisions about next steps in instruction that are likely to be better focused or informed than the decisions would have been without the evidence (Wiliam, 2011). Formative assessment implies a pragmatic intent—to improve the precision of instructional plans; and an immediacy—to improve those plans in the very near term.

In some school settings, the term *formative assessment* is used as a descriptor for purchased, standardized tests that are administered at intervals during the school year, scored by a test-scoring company, and returned to teachers for their use. The idea is that such tests help teachers prepare students for the year-end high-stakes tests. Without debating the merits of that latter statement, such tests do not fall within the use of the term *formative assessment* in this book. The competencies measured by those tests may or may not align tightly with goals of a written curriculum. Almost certainly the time span between administration of the tests and their scoring precludes immediate and frequent adjustment of instruction based on those scores. We envision formative assessment as a much more organic and persistent interactive loop between teachers' classroom observations and their instructional actions that develops their capacity to understand both content and learners more systematically and in a more multidimensional way. "It is the local cycle of performance and feedback that produces most of students' learning and most improvement of schools" (Wiggins, 1993, p. 18). Such classroom-rooted assessment professionalizes teachers as it benefits student growth.

Two categories of formative assessment are pre-assessment and ongoing assessment. As noted earlier, many people use the term *formative assessment* when they are referring to ongoing assessment. Although the two categories have a number of similarities, their timing and uses differ enough to support calling attention to both the similarities and the differences. We'll talk more about pre-assessment and ongoing assessment in the next section of this chapter and in upcoming chapters as well.

Summative assessment has a different tone and purpose than formative assessment. Whereas the intent of formative assessment is to help teachers and students change course when warranted to improve instructional outcomes, summative assessment is intended to measure and evaluate student outcomes. Thus whereas formative assessment should rarely be graded (more on this later), summative assessment suggests that a grade will be given and a student's performance will be evaluated based, to some degree, on the information elicited. Perhaps the most succinct and best-known distinction between formative and summative assessment was provided by Robert Stake (cited in Earl, 2003), who described formative assessment as taking place when a *cook* tastes the soup and summative assessment when the *guests* taste the soup. In the former, the goal is adjustment while there is still time to adjust; in the latter, there is a finality that accompanies judgment!

The When, What, and Why of Assessment

It's useful to think about assessment in a differentiated classroom in terms of *when* it should occur, *what* should be assessed, and *why* assessment might be used.

When to Assess

Effective differentiation requires teachers to assess student status before a unit of study begins (pre-assessment), throughout the unit of study (formative or ongoing assessment), and at key ending or wrap-up points in a unit of study (summative assessment). Pre- or diagnostic assessment helps determine a student's starting point with learning targets (KUDs) as well as with prerequisite knowledge, understandings, and skills that are essential to continued progress in a content sequence. Pre-assessment is also useful in developing awareness about students' interests and learning preferences. Formative (ongoing) assessment lets teachers closely monitor a student's evolving knowledge, understanding, and skills—including any misunderstandings a student may have or develop about key content. As with diagnostic or pre-assessment, formative assessment also plays a role in revealing students' various interests and approaches to learning. Summative assessment evaluates a student's status with the learning targets or KUDs at designated endpoints or checkpoints in a unit of study—for example, at the end of a section of a unit, end of a marking period, end of a semester, midterm, and so on. Differentiation places particular emphasis on pre-assessment and formative assessment.

Assessment in an effectively differentiated classroom will be both informal and formal. Informal assessments include things like talking with students as they enter and leave the room, observing students as they work on a task or in groups, watching students on the playground or at lunch, asking students to use hand signals or colored cards to indicate their degree of confidence with a skill they have just practiced, or making note of informative comments made by parents at a back-to-school night. Informal assessments are useful in giving a teacher a sense of what makes a student tick, providing a big-picture look at how the class as a whole seems to be faring at a given moment, and amassing a growing sense of how specific students work in particular contexts. They are not as useful in revealing the status of each student in the class with regard to a particular learning target or set of learning targets. Formal assessments (which we discuss in greater detail later in the book) include things like surveys, quizzes, exit cards, Frayer diagrams, quick-writes, homework checks, purposeful note taking about students' proficiencies, interests, or learning approaches, and so on. Unlike informal assessments, formal assessments generally provide data from all students on a particular learning target or set of learning targets that a teacher can systematically study for purposes of instructional decision making—and that a student can examine relative to important learning goals.

What to Assess

Students vary in at least three ways that affect learning: readiness, interest, and learning profile. As we noted in Chapter 1, readiness has to do with a student's current proximity to current learning targets (KUDs); interest has to do with topics, ideas, or skills that attract a student, generate enthusiasm, or align with a student's passion; and learning profile relates to a preferred mode of learning or learning preference. Teachers can better focus their planning if they understand their students' differences in these areas; therefore, teachers should assess all three. Of the three, understanding student readiness calls for more persistent assessment and analysis of assessment information in order to plan curriculum and instruction that moves each student forward from his current point of entry.

Why Assess

Various experts use three different prepositions to suggest purposes of assessment. They distinguish between assessment *of* instruction, assessment *for* instruction, and assessment *as* instruction (Chappius, Stiggins, Chappius, & Arter, 2012; Earl, 2003).

Assessment *of* instruction is summative and is especially useful in determining the degree to which a student has mastered an extended body of content or set of KUDs at a concluding point in a sequence of learning. Summative assessments result in grades that should reveal that degree of mastery.

Assessment *for* instruction emphasizes a teacher's use of information derived from assessments to do instructional planning that can effectively and efficiently move students ahead from their current points of knowledge, understanding, and skill. Assessment *for* instruction can also be useful in understanding and addressing students' interests and approaches to learning. Assessment *for* learning should rarely be graded. Feedback that helps students clearly understand areas of proficiency and areas that need additional attention is generally more useful than grading because students are still practicing and refining competencies, and premature grading or judgment creates an environment that feels unsafe for students to engage in learning.

Assessment *as* instruction is targeted at ensuring that assessment becomes a key part of teaching and learning. Its aim is to help students compare their work on assessments to specified learning targets so they become more aware of their own growth relative to important learning targets (KUDs) and develop the skills necessary to enhance their own success with the content, and to help their peers do so as well.

A Game Plan for Assessment

Teachers who consistently use pre-assessment and ongoing, or formative, assessment ask themselves a series of questions as they plan curriculum, assessment, and instruction. The questions both inform teachers' thinking about the nature of teaching and learning and their instructional planning and provide a sort of game plan for unifying or aligning what the teacher teaches, what the teacher assesses, and what the teacher positions as central in the teaching-learning process. The questions and brief explanations follow.

- *What are the learning targets (KUDs) for this unit or learning experience?* A hand-in-glove relationship should exist between learning targets, assessments (both formative and summative), and instruction. That relationship stems from a teacher's clear and vital understanding of how a discipline or content area is organized to make sense. That understanding points a teacher to the knowledge that is necessary for literate and informed interaction with the content, to the principles or big ideas around which a topic pivots (understandings), and to the skills a student must have or develop in order to use critical knowledge or act on central understandings. These KUDs not only form the framework of the unit content, but also clearly indicate the focus of pre-assessment, formative assessment, and summative assessment, as well as defining the core of instruction. Without clear KUDs, curriculum, assessment, and instruction lack a rudder.

- *What is the most essential knowledge, understanding, and skill for students to master in this unit or learning experience?* A teacher could teach scores if not hundreds or thousands of things in any unit of study. These things are not of equal value in helping students develop competence and confidence in the discipline or content area. Curriculum races—the dash to cover a mound of material in a short time—are not brain friendly. They neither engage learners nor lead to understanding. Effective teaching is predicated upon a teacher's ability to focus on what matters most, and to help students do the same (National Research Council, 2001; Sousa & Tomlinson, 2011; Wiggins & McTighe, 1998).

- *Which of those essentials are the focus of today's lesson and should therefore be the focus of the formative assessment that reflects the lesson?* A unit plan provides a range of essential knowledge, understanding, and skill that reflects the scope of the unit of study. Each lesson in the unit subdivides the KUDs to reflect the appropriate center of gravity of that lesson. Clarity about KUDs is essential at both the unit and lesson levels for focused teaching. It is equally critical for focused use of assessment to monitor the degree to which students are becoming proficient with what matters most in the content. It is not the goal of a pre-assessment or a formative assessment to check on everything in the unit, but rather to see how students are faring with the essential KUDs.

- *What strategies and mechanisms can I use to best determine student status relative to essential knowledge, understanding, and skill?* Many strategies are available for pre-assessment and formative assessment: quick notes taken while watching students work on an assignment, journal entries, short-answer quizzes, thumbs-up/thumbs-down signals from students, entry cards, exit cards, scanning student writing for particular traits, and so on. What makes one strategy better than another is not the strategy itself, but the match between the strategy and the assessment context—what the teacher needs to assess, the length of time appropriate for the assessment, and the time available for reviewing the assessment and planning instruction. Further, one strategy may be quite effective in assessing student mastery of information, whereas another would be distinctly preferable for assessing a student's ability to transfer a complex skill.

- *What prerequisite skills am I assuming students have as we enter the unit or learning experience?* A middle school teacher recently exhorted in a group of peers that he was increasingly annoyed by students who didn't know important things from the previous year's course in science. "I just don't understand what the lamebrain teacher was doing if kids don't know those things," he complained. After a pause, he added, "I've found that to be particularly confounding this year, because I'm the lamebrain that taught them last year." We've all been astonished that we have students who seem never to have heard of adjectives or who have no idea how to divide fractions or who don't know how to create perspective in a drawing when we know they've been taught those things on multiple occasions. Many teachers would be aghast if they were aware of the number of students who don't read proficiently enough to handle the course text. It's wise not to take for granted that students will bring to class with them foundational knowledge, understanding, and skill. Be specific about what you assume students know, understand, and can do. Then use pre-assessment and formative assessment to "test" those assumptions.

- *Where is each student in relation to the KUDs and prerequisite skills at this point?* Once you're clear on the KUDs for a unit or a particular segment of learning, create an assessment that reflects those KUDs and critical prerequisites. Check to determine each student's status with each KUD component.

- *How will I think about or organize what I see on the assessment?* Are you looking at today's assessment to see whether the student has the basic facts, can defend a position, can interpret an abstract idea, can transfer a skill into an unfamiliar setting, can interpret a graph? Perhaps it's important in the unit pre-assessment to note that some students can define three key terms and apply them, that some students can define the terms but not apply them, that some students can do a little (but not enough) of both, and that some students can do neither. Perhaps it's important to note that some students can replicate solving a math problem that was part of today's lesson but cannot explain how they did so. Pre-assessment and formative assessment are not about assigning grades but rather about detecting patterns. Once again, this is shaped by a teacher's clarity about content and its organization.

- *What am I going to do with the information I get from the assessment to move everyone forward in knowledge, understanding, and skills?* This is the "what next?" question. If I have students who have mastered telling time by the half hour or quarter hour, what's next? If I have students who've already mastered estimating time before I taught it, what do I do to make good use of their time while most students practice that skill? If a few students have no idea what agriculture is, how will I ensure that they are prepared to relate to the upcoming unit on the agricultural revolution? If some of my students already demonstrate knowledge acquisition and application, how do I guide them to be able to transfer what they've learned—or even to create with it? If four students can't summarize text, what do I need to do to teach them that skill, despite the fact that it's assumed to be a skill they acquired three years ago? Answering "What next?" calls on teachers to know sequences of learning in terms of knowledge, understanding, and skill; to locate students in those sequences; and to be prepared to move forward or backward in the sequences to help students find their next steps in learning. "Teachers [need to] know the learning intentions of their lessons, know how well they are attaining these criteria for all students, and know where to go next in light of the gap between students' current knowledge and understanding and the criteria for success for the lesson/unit" (Hattie, 2009, p. 239).

- *How will I keep track of everyone's progress?* It is not an assumption in a differentiated classroom that every student will always work on exactly the same knowledge, understanding, or skill at precisely the same time. What sort of checklist or matrix might a teacher create to list critical KUDs so that it's easy to note student mastery or difficulties as they arise? Does it make sense to have notebooks with a section for each student and lists of competencies where the teacher can make anecdotal notes after formal or informal assessments? Is there a way to involve students in keeping records of their own development? Monitoring student progress when that progress evolves along different time lines is not difficult, but it does call for teachers to be well organized and to have clarity on goals.

- *How can I involve students in more fully understanding and investing in their own growth?* It's quite possible that some, if not many, students have a sense that both learning and assessment are something that is done *to* them in school. As a result, they come to feel little agency or efficacy in the learning process. A primary goal of school must be to have students take charge of their growth as learners with competence and confidence in doing so. Assessment, rightly used, teaches students about the learning process and about themselves as learners. When students are clear about learning targets and have the opportunity to regularly compare their work to those targets, when they get meaningful feedback from teachers and make plans to act on that feedback, when they see evidence that their action results in improved work, they are developing a growth mindset and corresponding motivation to continue to work hard on their own behalf. Students of all ages should have regular experience in understanding and articulating the learning loop: "Here are my learning targets. Here are the strengths of my work. Here are the areas in which I still need to grow. Here's how I can do that both in class and at home. Here's how I'll know what progress I'm making as a result of my efforts." The power of assessment is magnified when teachers use it not only to inform their own teaching, but also to inform each student's learning.

• *How can assessment help students better understand how differentiation works?* In most classes that are effectively differentiated, the teacher mindfully builds a partnership of understanding and practice with students (Tomlinson & Imbeau, 2013). The message from teacher to students is this: "I want this year to be a great one for you, and to make that happen I need to know you well so I can always help you take your next steps in learning. That means I'll try to learn about you as eagerly as I try to learn about the ideas we'll share in class. It also means I'll need you to help me know what works for you as a learner and to help with the classroom processes and practices that allow me to work with all of the students in our class in ways that make sense for them." As the teacher both speaks and enacts the message throughout the year, students should come to understand that they are important to the teacher as individuals, that the teacher is continually working to understand where each student is relative to important goals, and that the teacher acts upon what she learns about students to create opportunities that help them grow from their current points of development, in ways that support their learning, and often in connection with something they care about. In that process, students come to understand that assessment helps the teacher understand their next steps, their interests, and their approaches to learning. When the teacher asks students to do varied assignments, tasks aren't determined based on who a teacher likes best or who a teacher thinks is smart or not smart. Rather, the assignments stem from the teacher's assessments—both formal and informal—of each student's progression toward clearly defined outcomes. Those same clearly defined outcomes also assist students in helping one another move ahead academically. The mutually understood and shared journey of growth provides a common rationale for shared efforts in establishing and maintaining orderly, flexible classroom routines.

Links Between Assessment
and Other Classroom Elements

It should be evident by now that curriculum and assessment are firmly linked because the KUDs established as the key learning targets for the curriculum will be what's assessed, both formatively and summatively. In turn, information about student progress gleaned from formative assessments, and to some degree from summative assessments, enables teachers to plan instruction that supports student growth with the KUDs from their current points of mastery. An important connection also links assessment and "teaching up," one of the principles of quality curriculum. Systematic monitoring of student growth examined against clear and rigorous learning goals (KUDs) should lead to systematic improvement of student performance so that goals "once thought very high and reachable by only a few become reasonable expectations for many students" (Wiggins, 1998, p. 12).

An effectively differentiated classroom also demonstrates important connections between assessment and learning environment, and between assessment and classroom leadership/management. When teachers regularly use assessment to help students develop competence and a sense of autonomy rather than to judge them, the environment feels safer and more predictable to students. When teachers help students understand that differentiated tasks often stem from assessment information, students come to understand that the teacher's goal is to help each learner take the next appropriate step in learning. This awareness is key to students' understanding of and contribution to the philosophy of differentiation that is central to a shared vision of the classroom and to managing routines that support student success in learning. With clear and dynamic learning goals, student progress monitored by persistent formative assessment, and instruction tailored to extend the likelihood that each student will develop proficiencies necessary for growth, a student's prospects for success are greatly enhanced when the summative or more judgmental aspects of assessment are in play.

3

Pre-assessment: Knowing Where Students Are as a Unit Begins

The most important single factor influencing learning is what the student already knows. Ascertain this and teach him accordingly.

—David Ausubel , *Educational Psychology: A Cognitive View*

A colleague shared a story about her unfortunate initiation to swimming. At her first swimming lesson, the swim coach asked the children to line up on the side of the pool in one of three groups. "If you don't yet know how to swim, line up here," he said, pointing to the shallow end of the pool. "If you know how to stay afloat but aren't yet comfortable with swimming strokes, line up here," he continued, as he pointed to a stripe near the center of the pool. "And if you are already a confident swimmer," he concluded, "line up here near the diving board." Our colleague's dad had told her repeatedly throughout her early years that she could do whatever she wanted to do in life. At that moment, she wanted to be a confident swimmer, so she joined the group of children near the diving board. When the coach asked that group to jump in the water and swim, she had a quick lesson in gravity, and the coach—dressed in slacks, a polo shirt, and running shoes—had to jump in the water to fish her out.

In retrospect, the story is humorous. It was not funny to the aspiring young swimmer at the time, however. The humor is also lost on many students in many classrooms many times a year who find themselves sinking beneath curriculum that is, at that moment, too deep for their current skills, and on students who are ready to swim competitively and who are asked to stand in the shallow end of the pool while less experienced classmates learn to put their faces in the water.

A teacher who consistently and effectively uses pre-assessment makes an implicit statement that she has no intention of "delivering curriculum" without understanding the entry points her varied learners will bring to the content she will commend to them.

Pre-assessment helps the teacher locate the "area of the pool" appropriate for each student as a unit of study is about to begin.

Informal pre-assessment of students can take at least two paths. One occurs as a teacher observes or talks with students at the outset of a school year and in the weeks and months that follow in ways that inform how she will shape and differentiate a unit. For example, a 3rd grade teacher who learns that she has seven students with a keen interest in dogs may offer the option of interviewing a veterinarian or a person who shows dogs when students conduct interviews as a basis for biographical writing they will do. As a social studies unit begins, a middle school teacher may conduct a somewhat more formal, but still indirect, pre-assessment of student comfort with a topic by asking students to use hand signals to rate themselves a one, two, or three in their comfort with using latitude and longitude to locate places. Both approaches give the teacher information that is potentially useful in planning for instruction, but neither is likely to provide information that is as systematic or available for study and review as more formal approaches to pre-assessment in which a teacher elicits or examines student work. For the specific purpose of identifying students' entry points, this sort of informal or indirect pre-assessment should be part of the fabric of differentiation—a teacher continually on the lookout for information that not only will provide some guidance for planning upcoming units of study, but also will help the teacher understand, connect with, and engender trust from students. Informal or indirect pre-assessment is less common than indirect or informal ongoing assessment, which we address more fully in Chapter 4.

In this chapter we examine more formal or direct pre-assessments of student readiness, interests, and learning profiles by providing explanations and examples for each category. We also explore the important question of how to make sense of and use pre-assessment information for instructional planning.

Back to the KUDs

At the outset of a discussion on planning pre-assessments, it's difficult to overemphasize the importance of teacher clarity about what students should know, understand, and be able to do as the result of a unit of study. Although it's not the goal of a pre-assessment to probe every piece of knowledge, understanding, and skill designated for an upcoming unit of study (or every relevant instance of prerequisite knowledge, understanding, and skill), it does matter to sample what's most pivotal in the unit. Therefore, before beginning to develop a pre-assessment, a teacher needs to be clear on, for example, critical vocabulary in the unit (an example of knowledge, or the K in KUD); foundational insights or understandings (the U) about the meaning or significance of the unit; and content skills that are at the core of what students will learn to do in the unit (the D). Skills should include not only basic skills, but also critical-thinking skills (such as application, comparison and contrast, supporting an argument, looking at events and issues from multiple perspectives, empathizing, noting flaws in reasoning, making connections across instances), and skills of a discipline (use of primary historical sources, scientific thinking, effective use of figurative language, mathematical reasoning, preparing a piece of art for exhibit). Content standards may provide direction in all or some of these areas. However, a set of standards is not, and should not be thought of as, a curriculum. Rather, standards are ingredients for curriculum. Dynamic curriculum requires a teacher who knows the content well enough to blend required ingredients (standards) with the nature and intent of the discipline in a way that represents both appropriately and that also helps learners relate to, organize, and make sense of the discipline's "narrative." In other words, the teacher has to know the "story" the unit is about to reveal for students well enough to have a good sense of what to sample in order to determine a student's point of entry.

Thinking Flexibly

It's useful to think about pre-assessment as a flexible process for extending a teacher's understanding of student learning needs rather than a fixed prescription or algorithm. Thinking about it in this way supports the need for insight to guide the use of pre-assessment. For example, what to pre-assess, how much to pre-assess, and when to pre-assess may vary with student background and unit requirements.

At times a teacher may only want to assess a student's entry point related to the unit's knowledge (Ks), or see how a student employs particular skills (Ds), or see what a student makes of a big idea or principle that will guide the study ahead (U). Most of the time, however, it makes sense to tap all three because they are all important in understanding students' varied starting points with the content of the unit and in planning comprehensively to ensure that instruction matches learners' needs. In brief, the first question a teacher should ask when composing a pre-assessment is "What Ks, what Us, and what Ds am I trying to measure here?"

There may also be times when a teacher wants to pre-assess for only a portion of an upcoming unit of study. For example, an algebra teacher wanted to pre-assess only the initial concept of a complex unit on quadratic equations in which she felt student understanding would be cumulative. Therefore, she decided to pre-assess the content for approximately the first week of a four-week unit, with another pre-assessment to follow for the remainder of the unit.

In addition, sometimes a pre-assessment is best administered soon after, rather than before, a unit begins. For instance, a group of kindergarten teachers felt confident that their students were highly unlikely to know much about symmetry and asymmetry before they introduced the concept. On the other hand, they also felt that some students might grasp the fundamental idea of symmetry quickly once they encountered it, while others might require additional time to understand and apply it. The teachers, therefore, agreed to do one lesson on symmetry and asymmetry in which they explained the terms and illustrated them with common objects. Over the next day or two, while students worked with other content, the teachers pre-assessed each student's understanding of the two concepts by giving each of them a bag with paper figures in it. Students drew three figures from the bag, explaining whether they thought each illustrated symmetry or asymmetry, and elaborating on why they selected their answer. The pre-assessment was much more revealing than it would have been had the teachers not introduced the concepts before the pre-assessment. As they listened to student responses and explanations, it became clear to the teachers that some students lacked foundational (prerequisite) vocabulary to move ahead with the ideas successfully and that other students' extensive vocabularies enabled them to deal with the concepts more rapidly than the teachers had assumed. The results of the pre-assessment guided teacher planning for students along a continuum of readiness to learn about and apply the concepts of symmetry and asymmetry.

Pre-assessing Student Readiness

Pre-assessment of student readiness has two functions. One is to provide the teacher with clarity regarding students' prior or prerequisite knowledge related to content that the upcoming learning segment is going to build upon. Assessing for prior knowledge can identify student misconceptions as well as gaps in knowledge and skills that a teacher might assume students of a particular grade level have already mastered. Although misconceptions and gaps can occur for various reasons (for example, incorrect prior instruction, the student's past experiences, forgetting), addressing them through targeted instruction is important because evidence suggests that students assimilate new content into their existing content schema (Tomlinson & Moon, 2013). If new content is taught without first identifying and then undoing misconceptions or identifying gaps in students' knowledge, understanding, or skill, misconceptions persist and gaps become gulches. Both inevitably interfere with intended learning.

The second role of pre-assessment of student readiness is to provide information for the teacher regarding students' levels of mastery of the unit's new content so that instruction can be appropriately targeted to their varied proficiencies with that content. It is important to not assume that students are blank slates or that because the content has not been directly taught (or because *we* haven't taught it to them) that students do not already have some level of mastery of the new content. To spend time reteaching concepts or skills that some students have already mastered is a waste of instructional time, just as it is a waste of time to forge ahead with new content for other students who enter the topic with critical misconceptions or significant gaps in knowledge or skill. Both cases result in little or no academic progress.

In addition to understanding the role a particular pre-assessment would best play for a given unit, teachers can use the following five quality indicators for pre-assessments as a guide.

Indicator 1: The pre-assessment targets the most important KUDs for students to develop and are aligned with current KUDs for beginning the planning of the instructional sequence. Here is a typical standard for a 3rd grade geometry unit: *Students choose and use appropriate units and measurement tools to determine the perimeter of a polygon with integer sides.* To pre-assess this standard, a teacher might give students a polygon figure with the length provided for each side. Their job would be to determine the perimeter of the polygon, and to both show and explain their work. In the example in Figure 3.1, students are not asked to define perimeter specifically, but rather to apply their knowledge of perimeter to solve the problem. The circle and the frame are distracters (because they are not polygons) that are added to identify any students who may not understand the concepts of polygon and perimeter. The directions also elicit procedural understanding about how to compute the answer. The question targets student knowledge (K) of vocabulary (including *polygon* and *perimeter*), their understanding (U) of how those concepts work, and their skill (D) in both computing perimeter and explaining their thinking process in doing so.

Figure 3.1
A Pre-assessment Designed to Show Students' Readiness

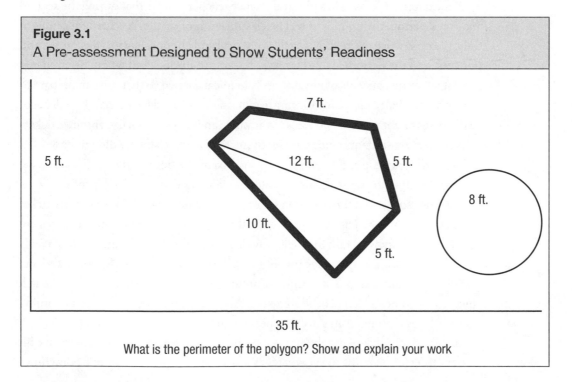

35 ft.

What is the perimeter of the polygon? Show and explain your work

Indicator 2: The pre-assessment uses a method that is appropriate for collecting the information the teacher is seeking to gather. If the goal of instruction is for students to develop an understanding of the scientific-inquiry process, one appropriate way to measure current levels of understanding would be to ask students to create a concept map that demonstrates the relationships among the process's different components and subcomponents that are provided in a list on the pre-assessment. If, however, the goal is to simply gather data regarding students' current knowledge of dates and places of Civil War battles, then the most appropriate pre-assessment method would be to ask students to indicate specific dates and places for certain battles—facts that could be gathered on entrance or exit cards or in paper-and-pencil quiz format. To the degree that teachers intend to teach for understanding, application, and transfer, pre-assessments (as well as formative and summative assessments) need to ask students to show evidence of those skills rather than only calling for knowledge-level responses.

Indicator 3: The pre-assessment recognizes time constraints. It's not necessary for pre-assessments to be lengthy in order to reveal what the teacher needs to know about students' current status with KUDs and pre-requisite KUDs. Often one or two well-designed questions or prompts are adequate. When a longer pre-assessment seems useful, questions can be given over the course of several days, a few at a time. In this way, the pre-assessment does not use a significant portion of instructional time in any one class period.

For example, Ms. Welsh, a physical science teacher, knows that during the second nine-week period, the unit focus will be classification of matter. As part of this unit of study, the class will explore topics such as physical and chemical properties, atoms and elements, and the periodic table. Ms. Welsh wants to understand where her students are relative to the concepts of physical and chemical change so that she can prepare to address her students' inevitable varying readiness levels. She decides that she will begin the pre-assessment process two weeks in advance and that she will use entrance tickets as the format. As students enter the classroom, they know to follow directions written on the board. They use index cards that are in a box by the door to answer the following question: "Define the three common states of matter and give examples for each one. If you are not sure about the common states of matter, just say so." This entrance ticket serves as an anchor activity before starting the day's instruction so that students are engaged in a meaningful task that will provide pre-assessment information Ms. Welsh can use in planning the upcoming unit of study. The pre-assessment is sufficiently brief that it doesn't take a significant amount of time from the day's instruction. She will repeat the entrance-ticket procedure with other questions focused on the upcoming unit's KUDs and prerequisites over the next several days.

A second way of thinking about pre-assessments and time constraints has to do with teachers' time for planning to use what they learn from the pre-assessment. Sometimes it's feasible to administer a pre-assessment on Tuesday, for example, and then to review students' work and use findings to plan for Wednesday's class. It's more likely, however, that the teacher needs more than one evening to review students' pre-assessment responses, digest what those responses reveal, and make sound instructional plans that incorporate those responses. For that reason, it's often wise to administer a pre-assessment a few days before the start of the new unit of study in order to deal with the constraints on the teacher's own time.

Indicator 4: Pre-assessment items should be ordered or arranged in a way that requires a minimum amount of time for the teacher to make sense of exactly where students are relative to the KUDs being assessed. Pre-assessment items can be arranged in several different ways to make it efficient for a teacher to make sense of students' entry points with the KUDs. One approach is for the teacher to "chunk" questions by topic so that those measuring common constructs are grouped together. For example, a teacher might develop a paper-and-pencil pre-assessment for an upcoming unit on force, motion, and energy. The first few items would focus on characteristics and interactions of moving objects (direction, speed, friction), and the next set of items would center on types of circuits (open/closed; parallel/series) and their functions. By grouping items related to similar content, the teacher minimizes the amount of time needed to get a snapshot of a student's degree of familiarity with each segment of content.

Arranging questions sequentially is a second way to maximize teacher efficiency in learning from student pre-assessments. This approach is particularly useful when attempting to assess student facility with a process, such as the writing process or the process of designing an experiment in science. For example, the writing process is often taught as a series of sequential steps that include brainstorming ideas, prewriting, writing, editing, and publishing. At the beginning of the year, a teacher might pre-assess students' understanding of the writing process by inviting them to write her a letter in their writing journals describing how they go about creating a poem or a story or an essay. Through this pre-assessment the teacher would gain information about students' understanding of the writing process and the structure of letters. In addition, she would gain some insight into the students as people—their interests, experiences, dreams, and so on—a vitally important aspect of studying and learning about learners.

A third way to arrange pre-assessment questions to facilitate efficiency of teacher review is hierarchical—moving from less complex concepts to more complex ones (see the example in Figure 3.2). Notice in the figure that the hierarchy of items includes prerequisite skills, skills projected for the upcoming unit, and skills that extend beyond the unit's skills in order to determine whether some students are entering the unit with skills that are significantly advanced. It takes only a short time to consider purposeful arrangement of questions on a pre-assessment.

Figure 3.2
A Hierarchical Pre-assessment in Math

Problem	Learning Goals
18 -11	Subtract two 2-digit numbers when the number is less than or equal to 20. (Necessary Prior Concept)
45 -23	Subtract two 2-digit and two 3-digit numbers when regrouping is not required. (Upcoming Unit Concept)
423 -222	Subtract two 2-digit and two 3-digit numbers when regrouping is not required. (Upcoming Unit Concept)
642 -430	Subtract two 2-digit and two 3-digit numbers when regrouping is not required. (Upcoming Unit Concept)
21 -17	Subtract 2-digit numbers with regrouping from tens' place. (Upcoming Unit Concept)
46 -37	Subtract 2-digit numbers with regrouping from tens' place. (Upcoming Unit Concept)
633 -327	Subtract 3-digit numbers requiring regrouping from either tens' or hundreds' place. (Horizon Concept)
552 -261	Subtract 3-digit numbers requiring regrouping from either tens' or hundreds' place (Horizon Concept)

When a particular arrangement reflects the content's logic, using such an arrangement can save considerable time as the teacher makes sense of pre-assessment results.

Indicator 5: The information gathered from the pre-assessment is used for the sole purpose of guiding instruction and is not used for grading or judging students. It's essential for students and teacher alike to be clear that pre-assessments are not used for grading students or for judging or categorizing them in any way. Fundamentally, grades are indicators of student proficiency after an amount of instruction and practice sufficient to suggest that mastery is a reasonable expectation. Pre-assessments are administered before either of those conditions is met and are therefore inappropriate for grading. Further, it's important to recall the interconnectedness between the five classroom elements discussed in Chapter 1. It is difficult, if not impossible, to create a classroom environment that feels safe and serves as a catalyst for learning if it is replete with judgments. Students who struggle with some aspects of a class need to be freed from the sense that each new cycle of learning reinforces their weaknesses. Those students need repeated experience with the message that learning is progressive and virtually always includes making mistakes that are important in helping students and the teacher figure out how to proceed in a clearer and more meaningful way. Students who may be advanced in much of a subject may well have come to value grades above learning itself. When presented with an appropriate challenge, such students may reject the stretch if they feel the risk will be punished with a poor grade if the product is not "perfect." Those students, too, need to understand the inevitability of errors and their instructive potential. For students to develop a growth mindset and to invest seriously in their own growth, they need to have ample proof that the teacher in a differentiated classroom asks for their consistent best effort, that pre- (and ongoing) assessments enable the teacher to teach them more effectively and enable them to contribute to their own success. They need to know that although there is a time in the classroom for summative demonstrations of their development, those come after multiple cycles of instruction, practice, feedback, and correction. A kindergarten teacher routinely reminded her students at the start of any pre-assessment, "I'm asking you these questions just so I can see what you already know and what I need to teach you so you can learn it. That makes me a better teacher and will help you be a better learner." That message is no less necessary for high school students—or students of any age.

Formats for Pre-assessments

Pre-assessment strategies can be indirect (informal) or direct (formal) measures. Indirect or informal strategies are typically unstructured in that specific instructional time is not devoted to systematically gathering the data for every student. Rather, the teacher conducts classroom "sweeps" or "samples." Examples of this type of pre-assessment strategy include, among others, windshield checks, thumbs-up/thumbs-down, KWL charts, and classroom-response systems (often referred to as "clickers"). Most strategies that are useful for pre-assessment are also useful for ongoing assessment. (See Figure 3.3 for descriptions of some indirect or informal pre-assessment strategies.)

One type of indirect or informal measure is students' self-reporting of where they believe they are relative to designated knowledge, understanding, or skill. The advantage of this approach is that it allows students to build self-reflection skills and it can be done quickly and with minimal intrusion on instruction. The major disadvantage is that the data are generally at the class rather than the individual level, making it difficult to get an accurate reading of the status of individual students. Further, students' self-evaluation may not be precise.

A second kind of informal or indirect pre-assessment is teacher observation of students. Very good teachers are also often very good student-watchers. As Mr. Arnold watched his kindergartners work with calendar math over the last couple of weeks, he

Figure 3.3
Indirect or Informal Strategies for Pre-assessment

Hand Signals—The teacher requests that students self-assess their own proficiency with knowledge, skill, or understanding in a particular area by holding up one finger if they're not yet comfortable with it, two fingers if they are mostly comfortable with it but still need to learn or practice more, three fingers if they feel very confident and could teach others about it. An alternative is to show a thumbs-up to indicate strong confidence, a thumbs-sideways to indicate reasonable confidence, and a thumbs-down to indicate that they are not yet comfortable or confident in the area.

KWL Charts and Other Organizers (Class Level)—The teacher conducts a discussion with the whole class on a topic about to be studied by having students contribute to a graphic organizer such as a KWL chart, in which students list what they already know about the topic (*K*), what they want to know (*W*), and, toward the end of the unit, what they learned (*L*). As the teacher hears K and W responses, she gets a general picture of student familiarity with the topic but not clarity about the status of each individual student. Other organizers such as concept maps or Venn diagrams are also useful.

Response Cards—The teacher poses a right-answer question to which students respond by holding up an index card with a preprepared response option on it. Each student might have three cards (such as *a*, *b*, and *c*) to select from, or two (such as *yes* and *no*). As students hold up their cards, the teacher quickly checks what proportion of the students have the correct response.

Informal Conversations and Observations—As teachers talk with students informally through the school day or formally as students work on tasks or in class discussions, and as they observe students informally while the students work, they become aware of particular students' interests, ways of working that seem to benefit some students or hamper others, topics or skills in which some students are quite advanced, or areas of deficiency for some students. This information can and should inform planning for upcoming units of study.

noticed several of them beginning to add the numbers on the calendar—including even some two-digit numbers. He began making a list of students who were venturing into addition so that he could follow up on their natural interest in addition in an upcoming unit on number concepts and operations. Ms. Lazen encourages her 5th graders to write daily about something important or interesting to them. As they write, she often sits and chats with them about their ideas and the ways they express them. She jots down on sticky notes things that seem useful and then puts the sticky notes on student pages in a writing notebook she refers to often as she plans upcoming units or lessons and as she talks with students or parents about students' growth as writers.

In both instances, the teachers' observations are purposeful and the teachers often use what they observe as part of their pre-assessment information. In neither case, however, does the teacher systematically gather the information on all students in a way that provides a complete class profile of relevant information for planning an upcoming unit.

Although both types of indirect or informal assessments—student self-reporting and teacher observation—can be used in pre-assessing student status and needs, they are better suited and more often used for ongoing assessment or formative assessment. We describe some additional strategies that are appropriate for ongoing assessment in Chapter 4.

Direct or formal strategies for pre-assessment of student readiness are structured moments when instructional time is given up for the sole purpose of gathering data at the individual student level across the entire class. Examples include paper-and-pencil pretests, preplanned and structured observations or interviews (such as think-alouds) with each student, graphic organizers/concept maps, problem sets, and journal entries, to name a few. Note again that most strategies that are useful for pre-assessment are also useful for formative or ongoing assessment. (See Figure 3.4 for descriptions of some direct or formal strategies for pre-assessment.) The key difference between indirect (informal) and direct (formal) pre-assessment strategies stems not so much from how teachers use resulting information to plan instruction as in the way instructional time is affected and the level at which information is obtained (sweep of a class versus each individual student).

Figure 3.4
Direct or Formal Strategies for Pre-assessment

Frayer Diagrams—A rectangle is divided into four equal sections, with an oval or an additional rectangle in the center. In the center figure, the teacher writes a concept or topic for an upcoming unit and asks students to share their current knowledge in the four quadrants, which are typically labeled "Definition or Explanation," "Information You Know," "Examples," and "Nonexamples." A nonexample is something related to the topic or concept, but not quite the same thing. For example, a whole number, a decimal, and a percentage are nonexamples for the concept of fraction. They are related, but not really fractions.

Systematic Observations/Interviews—The teacher has individual conversations with students or observes them systematically as they work or present work. The teacher records relevant information about each student on predesigned checklists or guides.

Journal Entries/Writing Prompts—The teacher poses a thought question central to a topic and students respond in writing.

Show and Tell—The teacher poses a question, and students both show (illustrate) and explain what they know about it. This approach is especially helpful in determining understanding for students who may be learning the language of the classroom or who have difficulty with written expression for a variety of other reasons, but who know something about the topic or skill at hand.

Student Self-Rating—The teacher provides students with a list of topics, concepts, or skills for an upcoming unit and asks them to rate their proficiency—for example, from 1 to 5, with 5 indicating that they are quite skilled or comfortable with it and 1 indicating they've not yet developed comfort or proficiency with the topic. For example, a world language teacher asked first-year students as the course began to rate their proficiency with subjects, predicates, direct objects, indirect objects, prepositions, and phrases in English or another language that is their first language.

Quizzes—The teacher administers and reviews a short answer or open response quiz designed to reflect the upcoming unit's KUDs and important prerequisite knowledge.

Interest Surveys—The teacher asks students to select from or rank options according to their interests, to list/draw and elaborate on their interests, or indicate certain approaches to learning they find to be particularly effective or ineffective for them as individuals.

Making Sense of Results

One of the most commonly asked questions regarding pre-assessment is "What do I do with the results?" The "now what" question isn't difficult to answer, but, as with many things in life, the answer isn't always evident at first.

The goal of pre-assessing is to understand where each student is at the moment with the upcoming unit's KUDs. Understanding what pre-assessment data can reveal about students' levels of competence with the KUDs or with prior knowledge requires the teacher to be a critical analyst. In other words, examining what each student has done on the pre-assessment relative to the KUDs helps teachers make informed, professional judgments about the degree to which meaningful differences exist among students. Meaningful differences are those that will affect the teaching-learning process. They are differences that suggest a one-size-fits-all approach is likely to miss some or many, if not all, students. Some students may lack prerequisite knowledge, understanding, or skill that is absolutely necessary for the work ahead. For example, understanding fractions is a crucial ingredient for early study in algebra. If students lack a solid understanding of properties of numbers and operations, the pursuit of the more complex concepts and operations in algebra simply will not be successful.

In other instances, some students may have misconceptions regarding KUDs that are the focus of study. For example, many students have the misconception that all rivers flow southward. This misconception may be a result of the way maps are oriented, or a confusion stemming from the idea that "up" is always north and "down" is south—another potential miscue from map orientation. Although many rivers do flow southward, the way in which rivers flow is simply a result of movement toward lower elevation. Lacking this understanding can cause confusion in working with maps, in social studies, in geography, and in some aspects of science.

Analysis of pre-assessment responses of still other students may indicate that they already have a sound understanding of content that the teacher is preparing to introduce. In other instances, the data may indicate that students have already mastered the necessary prerequisites as well as the new learning that is about to be addressed. For example, a pre-assessment for a mythology unit in middle school reveals that four students not only are familiar with many gods and goddesses in Greek and Roman mythology, but also can note parallel stories in myths from other civilizations. In addition, these students understand that myths mirror the culture of the people who told them. These students do not need to spend three or four weeks "relearning" what they already understand in some depth. Rather, the teacher might plan, for example, to guide them in comparing and contrasting myths across times and cultures and to unpack the nature of the cultures by making inferences from myths central to their development.

In the real world of the classroom, it's likely also, of course, that some students will demonstrate advanced development with the unit's *K*s but be unable to explain how the information makes sense or demonstrate sophisticated insights about the unit's understandings (*Us*); they may also lack some fundamental skills (*Ds*). In these instances, a student may need additional instruction or practice with some aspects of the unit's content and more complex work than many peers with other aspects.

As teachers see patterns in the pre-assessment data, they make the critical move from administration of a pre-assessment to using the results for instructional planning. Making sense of the data begins with a simple sorting exercise—sorting student responses' into different stacks based on *meaningful differences* related to the KUDs. Patterns that emerge will vary with the assessment, the topic, and the students involved. In some cases, a teacher may conclude that as the unit begins, students fall into four clusters, based on readiness: (1) students who can both define and explain an idea, (2) students who can define but not explain the idea, (3) students who can explain the idea but without use of clear academic vocabulary (explain but not define), and (4) students who can do neither. In other cases, the pattern may be simply this: (1) students who begin the unit with a foundational grasp of important knowledge or skills and (2) students who begin the unit without such knowledge or skills. In still other instances, the pattern may just be (1) students who have necessary prerequisite knowledge and (2) students who do not.

For many teachers, instruction proceeds routinely with the implicit assumption that the same first steps in teaching and learning are correct for the entry points of all learners in the class. In fact, that assumption is rarely appropriate, and in a differentiated classroom the teacher doesn't make that assumption. Instead, the teacher examines pre-assessment responses for patterns of strengths and needs related to KUDs that suggest teaching and learning sequences that would benefit some, many, or all learners as a unit of study gets underway.

Pre-assessing for Student Interests and Learning Profiles

In addition to gathering information regarding students' readiness to learn new content, pre-assessments can also reveal students' interests and can shed light on their learning profiles or learning preferences. Understanding students' interests allows teachers to make content relevant for students in order to increase engagement in learning. Understanding the students' learning preferences helps teachers consider a range of ways in which students can take in, make sense of, and demonstrate proficiency with important content so that the learning process is as efficient for students as possible. Attending to both student interests and learning profiles can help maximize learning opportunities for a broad range of students.

Pre-assessing for Interests

Two interpretations of "student interest" can be helpful in shaping instruction to be a better fit for more students. First, interest can relate to pursuits students enjoy on their own time—in other words, things like music, basketball, collecting coins, community service, archeology, gaming, and so on. Skilled and willing teachers can find many connections between the content area they teach and student interests. Math, for example, easily connects to gaming, music, a variety of collections, building, the stock market, and even poetry. The themes of literature are evident in history, current events, art, and music—and in the school lunchroom. Science is easily located in politics, community action, literature, and world cultures, to name just a few possibilities. Teachers who talk with students about their own interests, listen for clues about students' passions, and directly survey (or pre-assess) student interests are well positioned to make links with students' interests in ways that greatly enhance content relevance, student motivation, and achievement. For example, students in an Algebra I class who worked with algebra problems personalized to address an area of interest performed better—particularly in more complex and abstract aspects of the content—than students who did not work with personalized problems (Walkington, cited in Sparks, 2012). Figure 3.5 provides an example of a high school pre-assessment of students' personal interests.

It's also possible to think of students' interests in a narrower but still useful way. By having students rank subtopics in a unit, topics in a yearlong study, or some other range of items required in a curriculum, a teacher gets a sense of which facets of study are more likely to be inviting to some students and less interesting or even aversive to others. With that information, the teacher can form expert groups with students who are drawn to a given aspect of a subject, enable excited students to share ideas with more reluctant ones, pay special attention to students whom the teacher knows are reserved about a topic, or connect a student's personal interest with a required topic in which that student is less interested. Figure 3.6 provides an example of this perspective on student interests. The teacher asked students to indicate which required genre they were already fans of, which seemed OK to them, and which ones they had negative feelings about. Student responses enabled her to pay extra attention to students working in a genre they didn't yet care for, to have students who favored a particular genre share their enthusiasm for that kind of writing, and to combine genres to address student interests as well as their reservations. For example, two students indicated a preference for animal stories and a distaste for mysteries. Working with the librarian, the teacher was able to find mysteries that involved animals and to add those books to the classroom library. Similarly, three students who didn't like fantasy enjoyed comedy. The librarian located fantasy books that included humor to add to the collection.

Figure 3.5

A Pre-assessment of Student Interests from a High School Biology Class

Directions: I'll be a better teacher for you if I understand some of your interests. In each box below, write an interest of yours. Write briefly about how you are involved with that interest. Note also any ways you can think of that the interest might connect with science.

Interest:	Interest:
Experience with it:	Experience with it:
Connection with science:	Connection with science:
Interest:	Interest:
Experience with it:	Experience with it:
Connection with science:	Connection with science:

Figure 3.6

A Pre-assessment of 2nd–3rd Graders' Interests Related to Genre

Genre Survey

Directions:

- Please put a star next to the genre that's most exciting for you.
- Please put a smiley face next to genres you think are OK.
- Please put a down arrow next to genres you think are yucky.

1. Historical fiction

2. Fantasy

3. Mystery

4. Comedy

5. Fiction about 2nd and 3rd graders

6. Outdoor adventure

7. Animal stories

8. Science fiction

Both approaches to understanding students' interests and connecting them with important content enhance student motivation to learn and therefore likely increase academic outcomes as well. Attending to student interest also clearly signals teachers' investment in their students.

Pre-assessing for Learning Profiles

Assessment of students' learning profiles, or preferred approaches to learning, merits caution. Despite ample evidence that individuals often approach the same task in different ways, experts in several disciplines are critical of how teachers assess and use the resulting information to address learning styles in classrooms. A number of experts (e.g., Coffield et al., 2004; Pashler et al., 2008) in psychology criticize the lack of clear definition of concepts such as "learning style" (in which they often and mistakenly include "intelligence preference") and admonish that the many different models of learning style and their varied emphases make the concept useless. Further, they are critical of educators' use of learning-style (and intelligence-preference) surveys to determine student strengths and weaknesses in this area because those instruments generally lack reliability and validity (Eliot, 2009; Salomone, 2003; Tannen, 1990; Storti, 1999; Trumbull, Rothstein-Fish, Greenfield, & Quiroz, 2001). Finally, psychologists stress that all individuals learn in a variety of ways, and that preferred approaches vary with time and context. Thus, they caution, labeling a student as being a particular kind of learner is not only unfounded but also restrictive. A number of neuroscientists are critical of the idea that individuals learn math, for example, by writing songs—a criticism of one popular use of Howard Gardner's multiple intelligence theory. Some sociologists condemn categorizing students as types of learners, pointing out that such categories often result in stereotyping and reminding us that labeling people is almost never without cost (Coffield et al., 2004; Pashler et al., 2008). At the same time, some neuroscientists (e.g., Willis, 2006, 2007) make the case that learning is both more natural and more durable when individuals take in and explore information through multiple modes and when students have opportunities to work in a variety of ways. Further, there is general agreement that gender and culture do shape an individual's approach to learning, but with the persistent caution that not all individuals from a given culture or gender will learn in the same way.

Best practice related to assessment of learning profiles and use of the resulting information likely includes the following do's and don'ts:

- Don't use instruments that lack evidence of validity and reliability to assess an individual's learning style or intelligence preferences.
- Don't categorize or label students as being a particular kind or category of learner.

- Don't always teach in the ways that are most comfortable for *you*.
- Do study your students to see what helps them succeed and what hinders their success. Take anecdotal notes on choices students make when they have learning options. Ask them to tell you which teaching and learning approaches in your class are most effective in helping them learn. Talk with parents to benefit from their insights about how their students seem to learn best.
- Do present content through multiple modes.
- Do provide opportunities for students to make sense of ideas and skills and to demonstrate what they've learned in varied ways.
- Do help students understand that they can learn in a variety of ways and help them develop awareness of when an approach is working in their favor, when it's not, and how to change approaches when warranted.

Effective differentiated instruction includes flexible grouping of students, consistent use of varied pathways to accomplish important goals, varied approaches to teaching, varied use of media to support learning, multiple options for expressing ideas and demonstrating learning, flexible use of time and resources, and so on. Those things can all be accomplished without using dubious assessment tools and without labeling students.

Using Assessment Information to Plan Instruction

As noted in our earlier discussion about student readiness, our best current knowledge of the learning process points to the reality that student readiness to learn particular content at a particular time is a central factor in academic growth. In other words, to help students make the kind of academic progress they need and deserve, it's essential for a teacher to understand and address student readiness needs. That does not suggest that every element in every lesson has to be a perfect match for every student, but it does mean teachers need to understand and be ready to address general sequences of learning, know where students are at a given time, and be ready to help students move ahead from their starting points.

The roles of interest and learning profile in student success are both similar to and different from the role of readiness. Differentiating instruction based on student interest and learning profile contributes to two important attributes: motivation to learn and efficiency of learning. Some students find "schoolhouse learning" worthwhile only when they are able to connect it to their own experiences or backgrounds or affinities. Some students understand academic content first or best when they can relate it to personal interests. For some students, having the opportunity to move around or work with peers or draw before they write opens a gate to academic engagement. For these students, the role of interest-based or learning profile–based differentiation is pivotal—in many ways not only as important as readiness-based differentiation but tightly intertwined with it. For other students, opportunity to connect learning with interests or to learn in a particular way is an enhancement to readiness-based differentiation. In either case, what teachers can learn about their students' interests and approaches to learning opens the way to designing classroom experiences that meet students where they are in order to move them forward.

Understanding that a group of students in a math class are fans of a particular kind of music, for example, might lead a teacher to have students compare the rhythms in that type of music with a contrasting type, using fractions to express the rhythms. In fact, a research study (Courey, Balogh, Siker, & Paik, 2012) found higher test scores in the area of fractions for 3rd grade students from a multicultural and mixed socioeconomic public school who worked with a hands-on music curriculum in lieu of some in-class mathematics instruction. Students in the music group studied music notation, fraction symbols, and fraction equivalence in relation to music twice a week for six weeks. Their performance with both fraction concepts and fraction computation was significantly better, with high effect sizes, than that of students who only had math instruction in fractions.

Knowing that the class contains students from several different cultures might help an English teacher select readings from those cultures to use in conjunction with *Romeo and Juliet*, a required reading in her class. Observing that some students in a class are reticent to participate in whole-class discussions might encourage a teacher to use think-pair-share as an entrée to a class discussion.

Rarely would a teacher conduct pre-assessments of interests and learning profiles at the outset of every unit. Rather, the teacher might collect formal data on these two areas once or twice a semester, build on that formal collection of information with careful conversation and observation throughout the year, and seek feedback from students periodically on what works well in the classroom for them and what other suggestions they have for a better fit.

Student interest is important in selecting examples, illustrations, and analogies that teachers might use in presenting content, in designing student work that connects with student experiences and aspirations, and in grouping students. Learning profile is important in selection of teacher modes of presentation, designing student work that enables students to explore ideas and express learning in a range of ways, helping students access content, and grouping students. It's important to remember that a key practice in effective differentiation is flexible grouping. In regard to readiness, interest, and learning profile, groups should change often and should include opportunities to work with peers whose readiness levels, interests, and learning preferences are both similar to and different from one's own.

Planning Assessments with Student Variance in Mind

An assessment (including pre-assessments, formative or ongoing assessments, and summative assessments) is useful only if it succeeds in revealing what a student knows, understands, and can do at a given time. If a 3rd grader has a sound understanding of the water cycle but cannot write fluently, an assessment that requires writing a paragraph to describe the water cycle will be of little use to the teacher in developing a window into that child's level of proficiency on water cycles—not to mention discouraging the student who both knows that she understands what's important about the water cycle and knows that her inability to write keeps her from revealing that knowledge.

It's not imperative to differentiate every assessment; however, it's wise for a teacher to consider the fact that it might be short-sighted to differentiate instruction to support student success and then neglect to attend to students' learning differences on formative or summative assessments that are key to successful teaching and learning. Differentiating an assessment doesn't suggest creating different assessments, but rather ensuring access of opportunity for all students to demonstrate their learning.

In differentiating assessments, one attribute should almost always remain unchanged across all versions of the assessment: the knowledge, understanding, and skill for which students are responsible. The only exception to this guideline relates to students with individualized education plans (IEPs) that indicate a different curriculum or a different set of goals for the student. In those cases, assessments should, of course, mirror the goals prescribed for that particular student rather than someone else's. Beyond that, it's fine to modify nearly any other attribute of the assessment as long as it helps students to access the assessment directions and items or increases the likelihood that they can reveal what they have learned.

For example, it might be helpful to some students to orally record or to use a computer to enter their answers rather than writing them by hand. Some students might benefit from directions written in their first language so they are clear on the nature of the task. Some students might benefit from use of more complex language on the assessment because that language is appropriately challenging for their advanced stage of learning. On the other hand, some students might benefit from a version of the assessment that is written in simpler language or in bulleted form because long chunks of prose are problematic for them. It probably makes sense for some students to have a bit more time to complete the assessment or to be given its parts one at a time so they don't feel confused and overwhelmed. The show-and-tell format briefly explained in Figure 3.4 attends to variance in students' language proficiency. It's even okay if everyone doesn't have all the same questions, so that challenge level can match student development—as long as both versions of the assessment measure the same KUDs.

In schools with a major emphasis on standardized tests, teachers are prone to conclude that their own assessments must always approximate the nature of the year-end standardized test so students will be "ready" for that test when it comes. Certainly it's wise in those contexts to help students learn how to do their best work on such tests. However, we ought not to lose sight of the fact that if all teaching is proscribed by the very limited and limiting format of a particular test, students' learning experiences are woefully restricted. More to the point, the purpose of the instructional cycle (including assessment) is to help students learn. If they learn better because of how we teach and assess them, it's likely they will fare better on standardized tests than if we insist on teaching them in narrow ways that are ineffective for them. When learning "works" for a student, that student is likely to enter a testing situation both more competently and confidently than would otherwise have been the case, and outcomes should be predictably better. Further, the student is more likely to find learning itself a positive experience and one worth repeating rather than avoiding.

Designing and Using Pre-assessments: A Quick Review

Figure 3.7 summarizes the elements and purposes of pre-assessment. It highlights the role of pre-assessment in determining student readiness, interest, and learning profile.

It is likely clear at this point that implementing a pre-assessment so that the information it reveals can be used effectively to make instructional decisions requires thoughtful planning by the teacher. Planning quality pre-assessments calls on teachers to answer the following questions:

- What are the KUDs—the essential knowledge, understanding, and skill that form the core of the unit?
- What prerequisite knowledge, understanding, and skill should students have in order to succeed with the unit?
- What common misunderstandings do students often have about the unit's knowledge, understanding, or skills?
- What questions can I ask that appropriately sample the unit's KUDs, important prerequisite knowledge, and common misunderstandings?
- What is a reasonable amount of time to provide for the pre-assessment?
- Should it be administered in one sitting or across several?
- How long before the start of a new unit should the pre-assessment be administered so that I have time to review it, reflect on it, and plan with its results in mind?
- Are there students who would benefit from differentiation in the way the pre-assessment is written, designed, or administered?

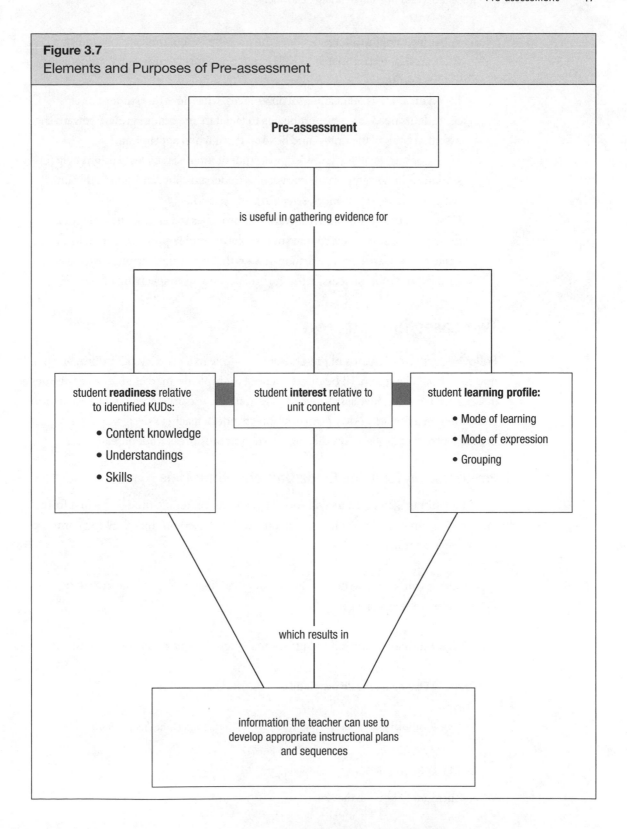

Figure 3.7
Elements and Purposes of Pre-assessment

Pre-assessment

is useful in gathering evidence for

student **readiness** relative to identified KUDs:

- Content knowledge
- Understandings
- Skills

student **interest** relative to unit content

student **learning profile:**

- Mode of learning
- Mode of expression
- Grouping

which results in

information the teacher can use to develop appropriate instructional plans and sequences

- What meaningful differences does the pre-assessment indicate exist among students in the class related to KUDs and prerequisite knowledge, understanding, and skill?
- Based on analysis of meaningful differences, what does this student or cluster of students need as a new unit begins to facilitate maximum growth toward the essential goals of the unit—and beyond them when appropriate?
- How does my evolving knowledge of student interests suggest I might help students connect important knowledge, understanding, and skill in this unit with their lives, experiences, strengths, and passions?
- Given what I know of students' varied approaches to learning, how might I design lessons and tasks so that students have ample opportunity to take in and make sense of what we're learning in ways that make the learning process more inviting and more successful for the broadest possible spectrum of learners?

Two Cases in Point

Following are two scenarios of pre-assessment—one in a primary classroom, one in a middle school classroom. (The middle school example on market analysis continues in Chapter 4 on formative assessment, to illustrate the use of assessment *for* instruction continuing in a unit of study.) Both examples model a teacher's design and use of pre-assessment with the goal of modifying instruction to address student readiness.

Pre-assessing for a 2nd Grade Unit on Telling Time

Mrs. Palmer's 2nd graders will soon begin a unit on telling time—the first formal unit on this topic for the students. The unit will be based on the following common core standard for mathematics:

Students will tell and write time from analog and digital clocks to the nearest five minutes, using a.m. and p.m.

Mrs. Palmer developed the following essential question and KUDs for the unit:

Essential Question: Why do people all over the world use clocks?
Know:
- Key vocabulary: *clock face, analog clock, digital clock, telling time, hour, minute, second, a.m., p.m.*
- Clocks help us tell time.
- There are 12 hours in the a.m.

- There are 12 hours in the p.m.

- There are 24 hours in a day.

- There are 60 minutes in an hour.

- There are 30 minutes in a half hour.

- There are 15 minutes in a quarter hour.

Understand:

- There are patterns in telling time and writing time.

Do:

- Tell time from digital and analog clocks to the hour, half hour, quarter hour, and five minutes.

- Write time from digital and analog clocks to the hour, half hour, quarter hour, and five minutes.

- Use *a.m.* and *p.m.* correctly when writing and telling time.

- Explain and apply the patterns in telling and writing time to the hour, half hour, quarter hour, and five minutes.

To pre-assess student readiness to tell time, Mrs. Palmer created a two-part activity for her students. She drew a large circle on pieces of paper for each student and asked them to use the circle to draw a clock that shows exactly 6 o'clock. She also asked them to use the back of the paper to tell what they know about clocks and time. Because her students had not yet formally studied time in school, she felt that the specific nature of the task with the circle and the open-ended task with writing about time would reveal prior knowledge some students brought to the unit as well as specific needs related to time that many students likely had. Figure 3.8 shows responses from six students in the class and clearly indicates a broad range of student readiness as the unit begins.

In reviewing the pre-assessments, Mrs. Palmer found some students who were unclear about the structure of a clock face, many who could accurately draw a clock face with hours positioned correctly but with confusion about the long hand and the short hand, some who could position the hours and the long and short hands correctly, a few who seemed to be aware of minutes but who could not place them with confidence, a few who placed them confidently but inaccurately, and a couple of students who could place minutes correctly. In addition, she noted a few students who provided little if any meaningful information about clocks and time, several whose information was accurate but limited, and several who appeared to understand the function of clocks with some precision, as well as writing time accurately and arranging events in a day chronologically. One student appeared to understand clocks and time at a level much more advanced than grade-level expectations.

Figure 3.8

Samples of Student Work on a 2nd Grade Pre-assessment for Telling Time

Kevino's Clock Face

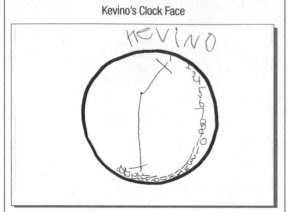

Kevino's Explanation

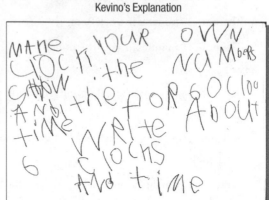

Shawn's Clock Face

Shawn's Explanation

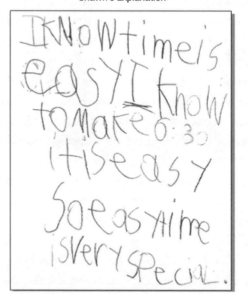

Directions for the pre-assessment asked students to use a circle provided to them to draw a clock face that said exactly 6 o'clock and to use the back of the paper to write what they knew about clocks and time.

Figure 3.8
Samples of Student Work on a 2nd Grade Pre-assessment for Telling Time *(continued)*

Tori's Clock Face

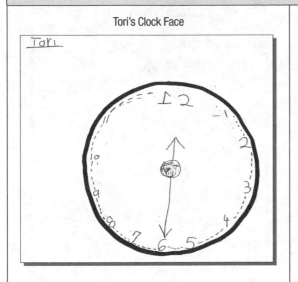

Tori's Explanation

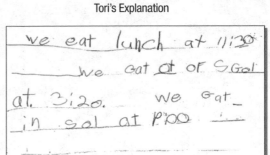

we eat lunch at 11:30
we eat at of S Gol
at 3:20.   we eat
in sol at p:00

Shaun R.'s Clock Face

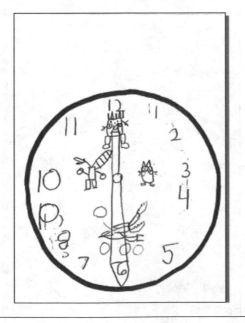

Shaun R.'s Explanation

6 o'clock   moms up
5 o'clock   DaDs up
7:15 Shaun R up
9 30 Kayll
8:30 Bad
9 o clock school
10:30 Snack
11:30 Lunch
4 o'clock home

Directions for the pre-assessment asked students to use a circle provided to them to draw a clock face that
said exactly 6 o'clock and to use the back of the paper to write what they knew about clocks and time.

Figure 3.8
Samples of Student Work on a 2nd Grade Pre-assessment for Telling Time *(continued)*

Chelsea's Clock Face	Chelsea's Explanation

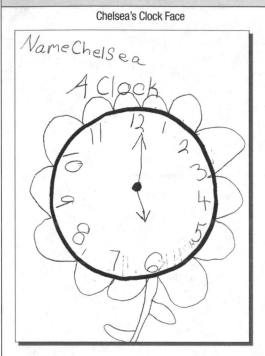

Chelsea's Explanation:

a Clock helps you tell time Clocks are fun 60 minit it 1 over I can Read from the Mikeerwada I wock at 6:00 and MY MOM was Lat for Work

Lianne's Clock Face	Lianne's Explanation

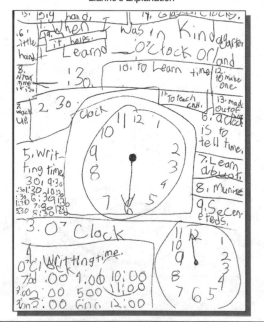

Directions for the pre-assessment asked students to use a circle provided to them to draw a clock face that said exactly 6 o'clock and to use the back of the paper to write what they knew about clocks and time.

As the unit began, Mrs. Palmer used the pre-assessment results to place students in center-based work that addressed their various readiness levels in preparing to tell time to five-minute intervals, using *a.m.* and *p.m.* accurately. At centers, students moved from station to station as their competencies developed. In addition, each day students played time games with a partner or a group of three at a similar readiness level. Directions for the game were based on students' current points of development with time. The class as a whole worked together on things such as "time mysteries," writing the day's schedule using time, and "setting the clock" as the teacher called on individuals to come to the front of the room to position the hands of a cardboard clock to a time she gave each student based on the student's readiness. They also listed ways clocks help them and other people (including characters in stories) go about their lives better. Subsequent formative assessments during later instructional segments helped Mrs. Palmer and her students understand and plan for students' growth in (and often beyond) the unit's KUDs.

Pre-assessing for a 6th Grade Unit on Market Analysis

Ms. Horner's 6th graders will soon begin a unit on market analysis. She knows that for students to have the best possible chance to really engage with the upcoming unit, she will need to organize the standards in a systematic and supportive way and to create a context in which the students will need to use what they learn in a way that is meaningful to them. She decides that early in the unit, she will introduce the idea of a performance assessment in which students can design and conduct a market survey, because that application of what they learn will likely appeal to her 6th graders. Throughout the unit, students will think about and prepare for the performance task as they work to develop and conduct a survey, hone their writing skills, and master the unit content related to probability. The unit will be based on the following KUDs:

Know:
- Key vocabulary: *random sampling, interview protocols, dividend, quotient, numerator, denominator, histogram, pictograph, bar graph, line graph, x & y axes*

Understand:
- Data can be represented in multiple forms.
- There is a relationship between fractions, decimals, and percentages.
- Specific sampling strategies increase the generalizability of the findings to a population from a smaller sample.

Do:
- Sample a population to answer a specific research question.
- Gather information by collecting data through surveys or interviews.
- Convert raw data to meaningful forms that require accurate calculations of decimals, fractions, and percents.

- Interpret the meaning and implications of data (words and numbers).

- Organize data in a clear, concise format.

- Represent data in narrative form.

Ms. Horner organized the KUDs and the related unit into four instructional chunks, as shown in the Market Analysis Unit that follows. To understand her students' starting points, she developed a pre-assessment to gather data for all four chunks. She opted not to use a multiple-choice format in order to eliminate the possibility that students could guess correct answers for some items. She also planned to gather additional data on students in each of the four areas through ongoing assessment once the unit began. It would have been possible for Ms. Horner to administer the questions related to each of the segments shortly before she began teaching the relevant segment. She opted to sample student proficiency with the KUDs for the whole unit at the outset, however, so she would have a big-picture sense of students' strengths and weaknesses, which in turn would enable her to pace the unit and to begin thinking about materials, instruction, and student learning opportunities for the entire unit as the unit began.

Market Analysis Unit

Four Instructional Segments:

1. Data collection—sampling issues, interviewing

2. Data analysis—calculation of fractions, decimals, percentages; interpreting interviews

3. Display and reporting of data—bar graphs, line graphs, histograms, narrative reports

4. Interpretation of and drawing conclusions from data

Pre-assessment:

1. The figure below represents what type of graph?

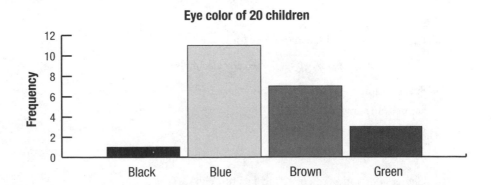

2. What does the graph above tell you about the eye color?

3. The number of repetitions of a short poem required for various students to learn to perfect recitation were as follows:

   17, 11, 10, 9, 6, 14, 10, 9, 8, 5, 12, 10, 9, 4, 11, 10, 9, 6, 3, 18

   Organize the data into a graph.

   $N =$ _____

   Mean = _____ (show calculations)

   Mode = _____

4. What percentage of students required 11 or more repetitions before perfecting their poems?   (Show calculations)

Convert the percentage to a fraction in lowest terms.

Convert the fraction to a decimal.

5. Which of the following is an essential part of descriptive research?

   a. random selection
   b. a sample
   c. a longitudinal approach
   d. an independent variable

Explain in your own words why you chose the answer you did in question 5.

6. Develop a hypothesis that can be tested by a survey.

7. Why does the A & N store in Seminole Road shopping center have different merchandise than the A & N store on the downtown mall?

As Ms. Horner reviewed the pre-assessments, she looked first at student responses to Questions 5 and 7, which related to the topic of data collection, and particularly to sampling. That was the first topic students would study in the unit, so she needed to quickly understand their various entry points related to this topic. She found that student responses suggested the use of two instructional groups: one with students who did not have a clear understanding of data collection and one with students who did.

As the unit began, she introduced the whole class to the performance assessment and the rubric they would use as a summative assessment, and she taught some whole-class lessons on sampling, developing survey questions, and designing surveys so that students would be prepared to begin planning for their summative task. Then she provided students with learning contracts in either blue folders or yellow folders. Contracts for students in the blue group focused on understanding and effective use of foundational knowledge, understanding, and skill related to data collection and sampling.

Contracts for students in the yellow group focused on random stratified sampling—a more sophisticated and complex application of data collection and sampling.

The unit segment on data collection and sampling lasted for five class periods. In the period before the contracts began, Ms. Horner introduced the contract to her students and talked with them about guidelines and expectations for their work. She also let them know that she would meet for part of two class sessions with the yellow contract group and part of two class sessions with the blue contract group. In those small-group sessions, she would do some direct teaching and also engage students in talking about data collection and sampling as it related to the requirements of their particular contracts. When students were not meeting with the teacher and did not have additional work to do on their contracts during the five days, they began planning for the questions they would pose on the survey for their summative performance task.

Both the primary and middle school examples presented here show the careful planning required to create and administer successful pre-assessments. Although such planning may seem time-consuming, the valuable information such pre-assessments yield leads to far more efficient and effective teaching and learning.

4

Ongoing Assessment: Knowing Where Students Are as a Unit Evolves

The only man who behaved sensibly was my tailor; he took my measurement anew every time he saw me, while all the rest went on with their old measurements and expected them to fit me.

—George Bernard Shaw

For several years at the University of Virginia, I (Carol) taught a doctoral seminar that involved content that was both complex and intense. The grapevine brought students to the class with high anxiety before I had a chance to introduce the class to them in an affirming way. Each week, students had to produce a paper that involved understanding the nature of an issue; finding, reading, and synthesizing current thought on the issue; and proposing a viable way of seeking solutions to the issue. Tensions were high each week as I returned the previous week's papers. If I waited until the end of class to return them, students had difficulty thinking about the current week's ideas. If I returned them as class began, it was nearly impossible for them to move beyond concern about how their grade stacked up against the grades of their classmates. I spent a great deal of time giving feedback on the papers, but, as is often the case for students, grades tended to trump comments.

As a new semester began, I found myself getting tense at the thought of the new students' predictable tensions and decided to make one "small" change in how I set up the class. On the first day, I told the students that each week I'd return the previous week's paper at the start of class with what I hoped would be clear, specific feedback on how that particular paper addressed the understandings and skills highlighted on the course rubric. I would give students 10 minutes to reread their papers, review the feedback, and write me a note indicating where they found the feedback to be clear, helpful, and on-target, and where they felt I'd missed the mark in some way. In the latter instance, I encouraged them to talk with me about their concerns—during work time in class, after class, or in a meeting with me. By the following day, each student needed to submit to me a specific plan for addressing the feedback in the next paper—in other words, to tell me what would be done to move ahead in areas that needed additional work. In the paper that followed, I provided feedback on the degree to which the students had carried out their plans, as well as continuing, evolutionary feedback on their reading, thinking, and writing.

I told the students I couldn't promise them that everyone would become a master craftsman in the skills on which the course focused, all of which were important in advanced graduate study; but I also told them that if they worked hard and were open with me in discussing their work, I could guarantee them that they would both understand what they needed to accomplish and would see noteworthy growth in their development in those areas.

At the end of the semester, I had students give one another feedback on drafts of their final papers. They discussed with one another how they would go about taking their final step for this class in what they were coming to understand was an ongoing process of developing and refining a demanding skill set. Ultimately, I asked each student to provide me with an assessment of the quality of his or her final paper using the rubric as a framework to guide the analysis. The students' self-assessments were remarkably on-target. When I returned final papers—with grades as well as feedback—no one was surprised or dismayed.

That semester will remain one of the most satisfying teaching experiences I've had in my life as a university teacher. The students were totally focused on learning and growing rather than on grades and status. Their clarity was greater about what learning goals for the class looked like and why they mattered. Questions were freer and more probing. The class felt safer. From the early days of the course until its conclusion, the students had a much greater sense of satisfaction and self-efficacy than had been the case in the past, and they were much less hesitant to acknowledge and grapple with areas of difficulty. The growth of both the individuals in the class and the class as a whole was noticeably greater than in past years. Further, the students regarded one another as partners in learning rather than as competitors, so that a growing sense of community developed throughout the semester.

In essence, the one "small" change changed everything. It freed us all to be learners and teachers who shared a common goal of developing significant competencies. The one small change, of course, was that formative assessment took center stage in the learning process.

The context of K–12 classrooms obviously differs in some ways compared with a graduate course, and yet the teaching-learning process is remarkably the same. In both instances, clear learning targets, regular coaching on how individuals can continue their growth toward—or beyond—those targets, and responsive instruction fuel learner success and satisfaction. In both instances, those conditions make teaching what it ought to be.

The Nature and Impact of Formative Assessment

Various experts on assessment define formative assessment in slightly different ways. Although the definitions emphasize somewhat different aspects of formative, or ongoing, assessment, they also represent general agreement on the nature and purpose of this powerful aspect of the teaching-learning process. Dylan Wiliam (2011; Black & Wiliam, 2009) proposes that assessments are formative to the extent that teachers gather, interpret, and use evidence about student performance to make decisions about next steps in instruction that are likely to be better or better-grounded than the decisions they would have made without the evidence. In other words, assessment becomes formative "when the evidence is actually used to adapt the teaching to meet student needs" (Black & Wiliam, 1998, p. 140). Wiliam also notes that equally important as *teachers'* use of assessment information to improve teaching is *students'* use of assessment information to improve their own learning or that of their peers. "Effective learners operate best when they have insight into their own strengths and weaknesses" (Brown, 1994, p. 9). Toward this end, formative assessment should be a frequent feature in classrooms, perhaps occurring two to five times a week in a content area (Hattie, 2012a).

Similarly, Lorna Earl (2003) defines two aspects of formative assessment, which she calls "assessment *for* learning" and "assessment *as* learning." In doing so, she also emphasizes the value of the process of formative assessment for both teachers and students. In discussing "assessment *for* learning," Earl emphasizes *teachers* building and using their personal knowledge of students, content, and the learning context to identify learners' varied needs and to use what they identify in service of the next stage of learning. In describing "assessment *as* learning," Earl notes that the *student* is the connector between assessment and learning. Students are not only a contributor to the assessment but also should become actively engaged in making sense of assessment information, relating what they see to clearly defined learning goals, and using feedback to monitor their own learning so they can make adjustments necessary to grow their knowledge, understanding, and skill.

Discussing what he calls "educative assessment," Grant Wiggins (1998) argues that such assessment is necessarily at the center of any endeavor that will markedly improve student performance. Educative assessment, he explains, is deliberately designed to teach and not just to measure. It provides rich, useful feedback to teachers and students, and it prompts use of that feedback to improve learning. It enables both teachers and students "to self-assess accurately and to self-correct their own performances increasingly over time" (p. 12).

The State Collaborative on Assessment and Student Standards (2008) adopted a widely cited definition of formative assessment as "a process used by teachers and students during instruction that provides feedback to adjust ongoing teaching and learning to improve students' achievement of intended instructional outcomes" (p. 3). This definition emphasizes two important points: first, that formative assessment is a process rather than a particular type or instance of assessment; and second, that the process starts once a unit of study begins and continues to unfold, following use of pre-assessment data that begins the unit of study. Thus, returning to Wiliam's explanation, it is *purpose* that makes assessment formative—gathering, learning from, and using information about student needs to adjust teaching and learning plans in ways that promise to contribute to student success.

A number of experts suggest that effective use of formative assessment is among the most powerful classroom tools for contributing to student achievement. As a result of his synthesis of over 800 meta-analyses, John Hattie (2009) lists effective use of formative assessment as among the very highest ranking contributors, with an effect size of 0.90. (He considers effect sizes above 0.50 to be worthwhile and effect sizes below 0.30 to be of little value. For comparison, consider the following effect sizes: ability grouping, 0.12; class size, 0.21; homework, 0.29; quality of teaching, 0.44; teacher clarity, 0.75.)

Noting formative assessment research from several countries, Black and Wiliam (1998) also point to very positive effect sizes of formative assessment on student achievement. They stress particularly positive effects on students who struggle with school and suggest that use of formative assessment to improve learning for these students holds particular promise in that it should reduce achievement gaps while improving achievement levels overall. We contend that effective use of formative assessment to help all students (including those who are academically advanced) succeed with materials and tasks that are appropriately challenging for them would result in impressive achievement gains across the board.

An examination of the impact of formative assessment on student achievement compared to 22 other approaches (including cross-age tutoring, increases in teacher education, teacher experience, summer school, more rigorous mathematics, class-size reduction, full-day kindergarten, exit exams, higher teacher licensure exams, and an additional school year) concluded that formative assessment was the most cost-effective in terms of boosting student achievement (Yeh, 2011).

In reality, judicious use of formative assessment is little more than common sense. If we want to maximize student growth, why would we *not* articulate clear and robust learning goals, teach with those goals squarely in mind, check the status of our students relative to what we just explained or what they just practiced, and do something about what the assessment reveals? This sequence of teacher thinking and planning is at the core of effective differentiation. It's simply fundamental to good teaching.

Although a predominant goal of ongoing assessment is gathering data to improve instructional fit for students, another important and related goal is use of assessment results for teacher reflection. In fact, Hattie (2012a) proposes that "feedback is more powerful when it is sought by the teacher about his or her teaching than by the student about his or her learning" (p. 137). Teachers grow as professionals when they examine assessment outcomes to (1) understand the quality of data obtained from the assessment, (2) examine the degree to which students mastered the instructional goals, (3) look for indications that there were misunderstandings or misconceptions created or sustained as a result of instruction, and (4) more accurately reflect on their own teaching effectiveness. Beyond revealing "right" and "wrong" answers, formative assessment data can suggest that certain instructional procedures were not effective, that student groupings were not the best fit for particular individuals, that different resources might have been better used, that the pace of instruction might have benefited from adjustment, and so on. In other words, effective formative assessment provides a two-sided mirror, providing insights about both the students and the teacher and indicating directions for the continuing development of both.

Formative Assessment, Grading, and Feedback

Although it seems evident that it's inappropriate to grade pre-assessments, it's more difficult for many teachers to relate to the advice of experts that ongoing formative assessment should rarely be graded. After all, that means we'd routinely give students in-class tasks that would not result in a grade. We'd assign homework with no intention of grading it. It's difficult not to hear ourselves saying, "But if we don't grade it, they won't do it."

In this case, it's instructive that students of all ages go to football or basketball or soccer practice, take part in swim meets, practice piano or drums or banjo, sketch, play video games, or take part in a myriad of other pursuits without anyone doling out grades along the way. Music students first work with an instructor who provides guidance; then they practice, get feedback and additional modeling and guidance, practice some more, and so on. Somewhere down the line, a recital takes place. The idea of the recital is to provide a meaningful setting for the students to demonstrate what they have learned as a result of the teaching-practice-feedback cycle. Basketball players likewise are instructed or coached, run through drills, and receive feedback multiple times over a week or two. No grades are involved; rather, the players play a game to use what they've learned through practice, knowing that the quality of practice is likely to affect the outcome of the game.

In virtually every learning context that is part of growing up, young people willingly—or with adult encouragement—engage in practice with the understanding that the practice will benefit them in an upcoming demonstration or application of what they've been practicing. Practice benefits the game, or the track meet, or the recital, or the concert, or the art exhibit—and feedback benefits the practice.

In classroom settings, we've lost two important elements in the practice-feedback-performance loop. First, we too rarely provide students with opportunities to demonstrate important skills in compelling contexts. In other words, we ask students to run sideline drills over and over without ever asking them to play the game (Wiggins & McTighe, 1998). Second, we've not shown students the connection between practice, feedback, and success "in the game." We can address the first omission by developing authentic assessments or student products that intrigue, challenge, and invite student investment. We can address the second omission by repeatedly helping students experience the reality that classwork and homework result in feedback that helps them do better and better work on subsequent classwork, on homework, and ultimately in meaningful performances—and on tests that are carefully designed to assess precisely what students have practiced. When grades are the primary motivator for learning, learning is diminished. As one educator noted, "If the question is, 'Do rewards motivate students?' the answer is, 'Absolutely! They motivate students to get rewards'" (Perricone, 2005, p. 68).

Routinely grading formative or ongoing assessments predictably impedes learning in at least three ways. First, it misrepresents the learning process to students, leading them to conclude that making errors is cause for punishment rather than an opportunity to improve (Hattie, 2012b). Second, it focuses students more on getting good grades than on learning. Third, it makes the classroom environment seem unsafe for many students—and would make it seem unsafe to more students if classwork were appropriately challenging for the full range of learners.

Rather than grading formative assessments, teachers need to provide focused, descriptive, and meaningful feedback on them. The word *feedback* was initially an engineering term describing a situation in which current knowledge about the state of a system was used to change the state of the system in the future (Wiliam, 2011). In a classroom, knowledge about the current state of student learning should be designed to help teachers and students understand how the student is doing along the way to important goals so that future learning can be affected positively. Effective feedback has the following attributes (Brookhart, 2012; Chappius, 2012; Hattie, 2012a; Wiggins, 2012; Wiliam, 2012):

- **Clear**—It's communicated in a way that the student can understand and relate to. (Example: "You explained the author's argument accurately, but you did not talk about the quality of evidence the author used in making her argument.")
- **Builds trust**—It's provided in a way that indicates to the student that the teacher is honest, cares about the student's growth, is invested in supporting it,

and trusts that the student can and will take action on the feedback. (Example: "Make a list of sources you'll use to show varied perspective on your topic, then check with me so we're sure you're on the right track before you move ahead with your reading.")

- **User-friendly**—It's respectful and takes into account the nature and needs of the individual. It describes what needs to be done rather than sounding judgmental or evaluative. (Example: "I can see progress in your use of sensory language in this piece of writing. As you continue to work with word choices, also include words that help with smooth transitions between your ideas and paragraphs.")

- **Specific**—It points students to precisely what they need to do to get better and articulates precisely what they have done well. (Example: "The explanation of the steps in your lab experiment is clear and easy to follow. You need to explain more fully why you drew the conclusion you drew from the experiment.")

- **Focused**—It's clearly focused on the most important KUDs at a given time. It helps keep the learner's focus on what matters most for the next step in growth. It's manageable in amount so that neither the student nor the teacher feels overwhelmed. (Example: "Think about organizing your ideas in a way that separates the comparisons you made from the contrasts. That will help your readers think more clearly. When you've done that, be sure your examples are all in the correct category of comparison or contrast.") If a piece of work indicates that the student is lost, *reteach*; don't generate a boatload of feedback that's likely to be both unhelpful and discouraging.

- **Differentiated**—It helps the student understand what her particular next steps are relative to important learning goals. (Example: "Your computation of area is correct and you effectively explained the process you used to solve the problem. To stretch your thinking, please create two minidisplays during math today. One should use addition and words to show why your answer to the problem is correct. The other one should use shapes and words to explain why your answer is correct.")

- **Timely**—It's frequent and is provided as soon as possible after work is completed so the student can act on the feedback efficiently. (Example: "Please use the feedback here to help develop a well-supported argument for tomorrow's 'cooperative controversy.'")

- **Invites follow-up**—The teacher makes suggestions for student improvement but does not do the work for the student. Rather, the student has the opportunity to take action on his own behalf. There is also opportunity for conversation with the teacher about the feedback and for the student to learn how to plan to use information from the feedback. (Example: "Think about why Gandhi is called a revolutionary in spite of his quiet approach to making change. Use those ideas to make your conclusion more powerful in explaining what made him unique.")

Feedback with these characteristics is far more useful in promoting learning than a score of *81* or a *D*- or even an *A*+. In fact, indications are that effective use of feedback can double the rate of student learning (Wiliam, 2011). Quality feedback that is routinely delivered becomes, a teacher might say, "part of how we do things in this classroom to make sure everyone grows and to make sure everyone knows how to grow." It also addresses Dylan Wiliam's (2011) important and often overlooked admonition that if we want feedback to increase student learning, we have to make sure that the feedback elicits a cognitive response from the student rather than an emotional one. In other words, the feedback should be designed to elicit thinking rather than defensiveness, anger, discouragement, complacency, or a host of other less productive student responses.

The Role of Students in Formative Assessment

As with pre-assessments, ongoing or formative assessments need to happen *with* students, not *to* them. That is the case for at least three reasons. First, a key goal of schools should be to develop autonomous learners—that is, young people who are confident and competent in identifying goals or purposes for learning; finding and using resources and experiences that can help them achieve the goals; monitoring their progress toward those goals; adjusting the learning process as necessary to revise or accomplish the goals; and verifying the degree to which the goals are met or exceeded. The classroom instruction-assessment cycle provides a powerful vehicle for teaching learners the skills of autonomous learning. Figure 4.1 illustrates how that might work as teachers help students develop awareness of learning goals, track their progress toward those goals, seek and use feedback to bolster learning, and appraise their success at key points along the way.

Helping students develop attitudes and skills necessary for autonomy as learners is also beneficial because it leads teachers to be more metacognitive about the teaching-learning process. That is, teachers must have clarity about the following: learning goals, why they are worth pursuing (beyond the need to pass a test—a rationale that is distinctly unpersuasive to many students), what criteria will indicate success, how to assess a student's current level of learning independence, and how to help the student move ahead autonomously while also helping the student develop important competencies in the subjects taught. Said a little differently, if teachers want to help their students become self-directed learners for life, then teachers will need to incorporate into their

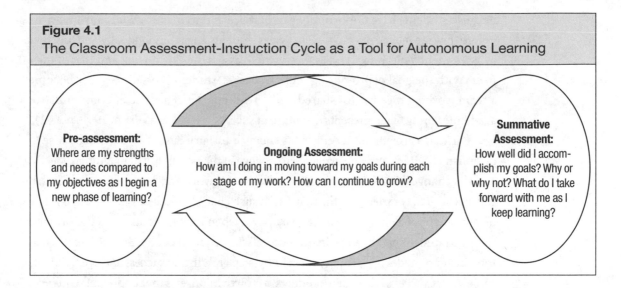

Figure 4.1
The Classroom Assessment-Instruction Cycle as a Tool for Autonomous Learning

Pre-assessment:
Where are my strengths
and needs compared to
my objectives as I begin a
new phase of learning?

Ongoing Assessment:
How am I doing in moving toward my goals during each
stage of my work? How can I continue to grow?

**Summative
Assessment:**
How well did I accom-
plish my goals? Why or
why not? What do I take
forward with me as I
keep learning?

teaching some *K*s, *U*s, and *D*s about learning, as well as *K*s, *U*s, and *D*s about history or music or science. Helping students "grow up" as learners while they "grow up" in content knowledge benefits learners both in mastering key content knowledge and in developing as human beings. Refining teacher awareness of how learning proceeds extends important skills.

Finally, teaching students to help one another in assessing their growth toward key content goals is beneficial on several levels. Students should become more aware of goals and criteria for success when they discuss the goals with peers and provide feedback on peers' work than when they focus on only their own work. Part of the increased awareness likely stems from a "rehearsal effect" of conversation and from a sense of responsibility for having a positive impact on a classmate's success. Some of the benefit no doubt also stems from the likelihood that the other student's work functions as a model—positive or negative—that brings clarity about one's own work and status.

Formative Assessment and the Other Key Elements of Differentiation

Think of the five key elements of a differentiated classroom—learning environment, curriculum, assessment, instruction, and leadership/management—as cogs turning together interdependently, with each one having an impact on the efficiency and effectiveness of the other four. Then consider the connections between formative assessment and the other elements. One of the most striking, and perhaps least anticipated, impacts of formative assessment is on learning environment, including student and teacher mindset. Formative assessment contributes to a sense of safety in a differentiated classroom because students have opportunities to practice and to make and learn from errors before they are judged or graded. Further, as students engage individually and together in assessment *for* learning, and as they learn to assess their own work and that of their peers with the goal of promoting mutual success, students and the teacher become a team working together for shared ends. They construct a sense of community or academic family that represents a "culture of success" (Black & Wiliam, 1998, p. 142).

Further, a growth mind-set is not generated by fairy dust or by a general sense of optimism. Students can't be expected to believe in the possibility of magnified success and the changes teachers ask them to make in their work and beliefs on behalf of that success until they experience the benefits of such change (Black & Wiliam, 1998). The development of a growth mind-set may begin when the teacher accepts the premise that each student has the capacity to succeed with required content, but it is realized as the teacher provides opportunity for step-by-step growth and success and sees students achieve that success. Likewise in students, a growth mindset is the product of sequences of success. Effective use of formative assessment is foundational to that incremental process of a student's investment of effort in practice, opportunity to learn from the effort and self-correct to promote investment of effort in the next practice, and so on. Formative assessment, effectively used, demonstrates to students that we are listening to them, want them to grow, and are providing specific support and guidance for that growth (Hattie, 2012a).

The relationship between formative assessment and curriculum is also clear and compelling. Without clear goals established in curriculum, formative assessments are likely to misalign with both curriculum and instruction. In addition, as Black and Wiliam (1998) note,

> Students can assess themselves only when they have a sufficiently clear picture of the targets their learning is meant to attain. Surprisingly and sadly, many students do not have such a picture .... When students do acquire such an overview, they then become more committed and more effective as learners. (p. 143)

Certainly it is the case that effective differentiation of instruction is inextricably bound to formative assessment. When teachers establish clear curricular goals and use formative assessment to understand the status of their students relative to those goals throughout a learning sequence, differentiation is simply what comes next (Earl, 2003). Further, unless differentiation is based largely on pre- and ongoing assessment information, it is an exercise in futility. As Hattie (2012b) observes, "For differentiation to be effective, teachers need to know, for each student, where the student begins and where he or she is in his or her journey toward meeting the criteria of the lesson" (p. 98). He concludes that it should be obvious that formative assessment with rapid feedback is a powerful tool for teachers who want to know their students and know how to help them achieve.

Finally, unless a teacher can help students understand the need to create a classroom that benefits the growth of all students and can establish and manage the routines necessary to allow flexible instruction, differentiation is not likely to occur, and the evidence of students' varied needs provided by formative assessment is unlikely to be used by teachers or students for the purpose of improving student outcomes.

Formats for Ongoing Assessments

As noted in Chapter 3, many formats that are appropriate for pre-assessing student readiness and interest are equally useful for ongoing assessment as well—for example, informal or indirect strategies such as hand signals, response cards, and informal conversations and interviews, and direct or formal strategies such as interest surveys, Frayer diagrams, journal or writing prompts, systematic observations and interviews, quizzes, and show-and-tell responses. Some formats are more often associated with ongoing assessment—especially of student readiness. Figure 4.2 lists and describes some direct or formal strategies most often used for ongoing assessment. Teachers should feel free to develop their own strategies based on the needs of their students, the content they are teaching, and the particular contexts of their classrooms. The examples listed here and in Chapter 3 are just a sampling of possibilities. It's important to recall that virtually all student work (including class practice and homework) can be used as formative assessment—a reminder that the format is not as important as the intent for and the use of what students produce. In addition, it's important to know that not every student assignment will be an assessment. Some, and probably many, assignments exist to help students make sense of critical content. Occasionally an assignment's purpose is to determine the degree to which the student has made sense of that critical content. In the former instance, the assignments are simply practice; in the latter, the assignment becomes a formative assessment.

Making Sense of Ongoing Assessment Information

As has been the case in other areas, many of the ideas discussed in this section apply to effective use of pre-assessment as well as to effective use of ongoing assessment. Successful use of information from ongoing assessments for instructional planning actually begins with design of the assessments—and to a great degree with curriculum design. Two key factors in understanding and planning from ongoing assessment begin even before administration of the assessment. Those factors are ensuring goal clarity and understanding instructional sequences.

Figure 4.2
Direct or Formal Strategies for Ongoing Assessment

Graphic Organizers—Students individually complete a graphic organizer on a topic or question posed by the teacher. The teacher reviews and assesses each student's work according to pre-established criteria to determine students' proficiency with the topic or question.

Exit Cards—The teacher poses one or more questions directly related to the day's lesson, and students provide brief responses on index cards, slips of paper, or sticky notes. Students hand in or post their responses as they leave the room or change subjects within the room.

3-2-1 Cards—This is a kind of exit card in which a student responds to questions or prompts that ask for 3 responses, then 2, then 1—for example: the 3 most important causes of U.S. entry into World War II, 2 ways in which U.S. entry into World War II was different from the reasons for participation in World War I, and 1 question the student needs to have answered regarding U.S. involvement in World War II. The card can also be arranged in 1-2-3 order, and a wide variety of prompts can be used.

Entry Cards—Students respond to a posted question as they enter the room and turn it in as class begins. Often the questions relate to homework or to an important element of the previous day's class.

POE Exercises—The teacher presents a demonstration, reads a passage, or describes a scenario, then asks students to write down what they predict (P) will happen next. The teacher then continues with the demonstration, passage, or scenario, asking the student to observe (O) what actually did happen. Students then explain (E) why their initial response was accurate or inaccurate.

Whip-Arounds—The teacher poses a question that is likely to reveal student understanding or misunderstanding but that can be answered in a sentence. Students have a couple of minutes to write their answer. The teacher shows students the order of progression in which they should share their answers orally with directions for students to read their answer in the designated order. As students read, teachers use indicators to note quality of response beside a list of student names (e.g., 1 = clear understanding, 2 = near understanding, 3 = weak understanding, 4 = no apparent understanding).

Windshield Checks—Using the analogy of traveling by car, the teacher asks students to select one of three windshield conditions to describe their current status with the topic, skill, or information at hand. A clear windshield indicates the student can see the learning target clearly and understands it. A "buggy" windshield suggests the student can see the target but lacks clarity on some elements or parts of the content. A mud-covered windshield indicates the student doesn't understand the topic or skill, or can't "see" it clearly at all yet. Windshield checks are a kind of student self-rating. Teachers may vary the analogy. For example, a "Weather Report" asks student to rate their proficiency with the topic or skill by indicating "sunny skies," "a few high clouds," or "fog and smog."

Homework—Homework should generally provide opportunity for students to practice knowledge, understanding, or skill that they have not yet mastered. In that way, it can provide important insight into what students do and don't yet grasp. Because homework is practice, it should not generally be graded, but effective feedback on homework can help students understand how to move ahead with learning.

Quizzes—Both short-answer and open-ended responses can be designed to reveal student knowledge, understanding, and skill at a given point in a unit of study. Quizzes should most often be regarded as practice and not graded, although it is acceptable to grade announced quizzes at "conclusion" or "check" points in a unit after students have had ample opportunity for practice.

Ensuring Goal Clarity

Effective use of ongoing assessment requires clearly identified and defined learning goals as well as criteria for success with the goals that are communicated to students before instruction begins. Having clearly defined goals undergirds everything that follows: selecting appropriate content, designing learning activities to make the content accessible to students, and developing and interpreting assessments used throughout the instructional cycle. When goals are unclear or insipid, teaching is poorly focused, learning is diminished, and assessment information that should inform instruction is relatively useless.

Initially, it's important for teachers to be able to distinguish between and develop KUDs—goal statements for knowledge, understanding, and skill. As we've discussed before, *K*s are facts, vocabulary, names, dates, places, lists, procedures—generally information that learners must commit to memory. Here is an example of a *K* statement in health: "Students will know the components of fitness."

A *U* statement reveals how a particular idea makes sense, why we learn it, or how the idea works. It sparks insight and helps make meaning of content. A *U* statement should begin with the stem "I want my students to understand that . . . ." The stem does not have to appear in the *U* statement, but the statement should be written so that the stem can be placed in front of it. A statement that begins with the stem "I want my students to understand how . . ." or "I want my students to understand why . . ." isn't really an understanding because the statement leaves it to the student to figure out the insight or meaning, which, of course, can result in many students missing the point. Content standards that focus on understanding may or may not be written as effective *U* statements. When they are not, it's important for the teacher to translate the standard into language that reveals the insight or essential truth clearly. Here are some examples of essential understandings or *U* statements in health: "(I want my students to understand that) A body is a system that functions with interdependent parts"; "(I want my students to understand that) Forces that affect the body system include environmental, genetic, and lifestyle factors."

Skills are mental or physical actions students should be able to perform or do, and *D* statements are typically verbs or verb phrases that include the skill, or *D*, but do not describe a specific instructional activity. The *D*s can and should include basic skills, critical and creative thinking skills, skills of a particular discipline, skills of collaboration, production skills, and skills of independence (such as metacognition, planning, using criteria to assess progress, developing useful questions, using resources to find valid information). Complex content standards such as common core standards and International Baccalaureate standards call on most, if not all, of those categories of skill.

Here is an example of a *D* statement in health: "(Students will) Develop a fitness plan to improve health for an individual with a specified lifestyle."

In a differentiated classroom, foundational goal statements (KUDs) do not vary across students except in the case of students with an IEP that indicates the student has learning goals that differ from age-mates in one or more areas. Differentiation provides different pathways and support systems for academically diverse students to achieve the same KUDs, and KUDs should have a high enough ceiling of expectation to make room for the full range of learners in a classroom. In other words, KUDs should incorporate essential knowledge important for all students to master in order to be literate in the content area or unit of study, understandings that help students see how the content makes sense and why it matters, and skills that are necessary to act upon, apply, transfer, or create with the understandings. Rich KUDs can be accessed at different levels of sophistication. For example, the KUDs that Matthew Reames, a former math teacher and a doctoral student at the University of Virginia at the time we were writing this book, developed for a math unit on geometry included the following essential or guiding question: "How might we describe the world around us?" Two of the unit understandings were (1) "Measurement is a way of describing the world numerically" and (2) "Units of measurement give us a standard way of describing the world." Students can approach both the essential question and the two understandings (the *U*s) at very specific and exploratory levels and at quite abstract and sophisticated levels—and at multiple degrees of complexity in between.

It's also important to realize that although a particular content standard may be written as a *K* or a *U* or a *D*, it's also possible for a single standard to incorporate or imply a combination of all three. For example, a standard from the National Center for History in the Schools indicates that students should know the major characteristics of civilizations and how civilizations emerged in Mesopotamia, Egypt, and the Indus Valley. Embedded in this standard is the knowledge that there are different civilizations (*K*) and the characteristics of the civilizations (*K*), as well as understanding how and why the three areas that represent the cultures became urbanized and came to serve as sources of cultural innovation in the fourth and third millennia before the Common Era (*U*s). To develop a full understanding of the standard, students must compare and contrast different sets of ideas, values, and perspectives as well as analyze causal relationships (*D*s). Teachers needs to be thoughtful and analytical in translating content standards to KUDs to ensure that their teaching plans assist students in developing critical knowledge and using important skills to arrive at, apply, and extend essential understandings. Formative assessments should monitor students' development with *K*s, *U*s, and *D*s—and their proficiency in using related *K*s and *D*s to make sense of, apply, and transfer *U*s.

Curriculum that is framed around KUDs is better organized for teaching and learning, more likely to be relevant to students, and more assessment-ready than "curriculum" that is simply a list of standards, the contents of a textbook, or a series of activities. (The latter three conceptions of curriculum, although common, are, in fact, significant misconceptions of what curriculum is or should be and diminish prospects for students' development as successful, motivated, self-guided, and sustaining learners.) Robust KUDs are the compass for planning meaningful formative assessments (as they are for planning meaningful instruction). At various points in a unit, students should be developing *K*s, *U*s, and *D*s, and formative assessments should, at appropriate points in the learning cycle, be monitoring student development with all three elements individually and in relationship with one another. Figure 4.3 provides an example of an ongoing assessment checking for students' understanding of the first part of the following *U* statement: "(I want my students to understand that) A culture is shaped by and shapes its geography, resources, economy, and lifestyle." To complete the assessment students have to illustrate or support their thinking with examples, which is a *D* goal. If we want students to understand and be able to apply, transfer, and create with what they learn, we have to assess for those abilities and place them at the heart of instructional planning as well.

Figure 4.3
An Ongoing Assessment in Elementary Social Studies

Mesopotamia

Directions: Select three of the elements and explain or show how they are related. Give specific examples to support your explanation.

Geography	Economy
Resources	Lifestyle

Understanding Instructional Sequences

Instructional sequences, learning progressions, or "ladders of understanding" (Popham, 2007, p. 68) are "a carefully sequenced set of building blocks that students must master en route to a more distant curricular aim. The building blocks consist of sub-skills and bodies of enabling knowledge" (p. 83). In most instances, students develop knowledge, understanding, or skill in a sort of stepwise fashion.

Thinking about instructional sequences simply causes a teacher to reflect on the question of an order in which students might most naturally and effectively develop a particular skill set or understanding or body of knowledge. Instructional sequences should not be thought of as rigid. Different curriculum designers would likely arrange a particular sequence somewhat differently. Further, different students might move to mastery in a somewhat different order because of varied interests, experiences, strengths, learning profiles, and so on. In addition, instructional sequences do not detail every small step along the way to mastering a body of content. Rather, they consider significant progressions or benchmarks that build toward proficiency with overarching ideas or skills. Figure 4.4 provides an example of a progression in number sense (based on Hess, 2010), and Figure 4.5 illustrates this in language arts (based on Hess, 2011).

Understanding and using instructional sequences or learning progressions invites a developmental view of learning that acknowledges that students do not all learn at the same rate, in the same ways, or with the same degree of sophistication. Viewing learning on a novice-to-expert continuum that builds over time rather than being constrained by a specific set of grade-level standards is a concept based on Vygotsky's (1978) Zone of Proximal Development (ZPD) as well as on our current best understanding of how the brain learns (Sousa & Tomlinson, 2011). In instructional planning for differentiation, a teacher would seek to help students move from their current points of understanding or skill to the next logical level of development. This kind of planning is fundamental to effective differentiation for student readiness and avoids the common (and costly) pitfalls of assuming students can skip steps in learning to function at "grade-level" expectations when those students are lacking critical prior steps in learning, or holding students at a particular stage of learning because "grade-level" expectations prescribe that step despite the reality that the student mastered it months or even years ago.

Instructional sequences relate to pre- and ongoing assessment in two ways. First, it makes sense to plan the assessments to determine students' status in a learning progression at a given time. Instructional sequences or learning progressions provide one way to think about assessing a student's prerequisite knowledge, understanding, or skill both as a unit begins and as it continues, and using the sequence or progressions as the basis for prompts on pre-assessments and ongoing assessments. In addition, of course, in making sense of pre- and ongoing assessment results, learning progressions can be valuable in

Figure 4.4
A Learning Progression in Number Sense (Based on Hess, 2010)

Course or Grade	Standard
Algebra II	Understand the hierarchy of the complex number system and relationships between the elements, properties, and operations.
Geometry	Establish the relationships between the real numbers and geometry; explore the importance of irrational numbers to geometry.
Algebra I	Understand properties of and relationships between subsets and elements of the real number system.
8	Extend understanding of the real number system to include irrational numbers.
7	Develop an understanding of and apply proportionality.
6	Understand and use ratios, rates, and percents.
5	Extend the understanding of place value through millions in various contexts and representations.
4	Understand place value of numbers from hundreds to the hundred-thousands place.
3	Understand the place value of whole numbers to the ten-thousands place, including expanded notation for all arithmetic operations.
2	Understand and use place value concepts to 1000.
1	Understand and use number notation and place value to 100.
K	Count objects in a set and use numbers, including written numerals to 25.

Figure 4.5	
A Learning Progression in Language Arts (Based on Hess, 2011)	

Grade	Learning Target
9–12	Identify and analyze how interrelationships of literary elements and point of view influence development of complex characters (motivations, interactions, archetypes).
7–8	Identify and analyze how use of literary elements (e.g., character, setting, plot/subplots) and point of view influence development of character.
5–6	Use evidence from text to support interpretations, inferences, or conclusions (e.g., character development, point of view).
3–4	Use supporting evidence to analyze character development and character traits (e.g., deeds, motivation, interactions).
K–2	Interpret and analyze literary elements within a text (e.g., intentions/feelings of characters, cause-effect relationships).

interpreting a student's current learning status and in planning for that student's next steps in learning. For instance, using the example in Figure 4.4, a 6th grade student who is working to master the grade 3 concept of place value to the ten-thousands place is highly unlikely to succeed with the grade-level concepts of ratios and percentages. A pre-assessment that revealed the student's entry point would be invaluable in helping the teacher provide focused instruction on place value—perhaps in small-group teaching, via a learning contract, at a math center, or through homework—to ensure a viable progression of understanding related to number sense. Instructional sequences or learning progressions support teachers in providing what Hattie (2012b) calls "deliberate practice at an appropriate level of challenge" (p. 110).

Unit design calls on teachers to think about a unit's meaning and about critical knowledge and skill necessary to illuminate that meaning, then to create goal statements that frame the unit by stating its essential knowledge (K), understandings (U), and skills (D) so that unit aims are clear to teacher and students alike. It calls on teachers to find ways to make the content meaningful and engaging for the students who will study it. It requires teachers to develop content, process, and products that focus students on understanding while drawing upon important knowledge and skill. When planning to differentiate the unit, it is important for the teacher also to understand learning progressions and to provide instruction and practice for students so that they can enter the study where they are and move forward logically and smoothly. Teachers who differentiate also account for ways in which they can connect content, process, and products with students' varied interests, and they create opportunities for students to take in, make sense of, and demonstrate their growth with the critical content.

To facilitate that process, teachers who differentiate instruction create pre- and ongoing assessments based on the designated KUDs for a unit while also accounting for essential prerequisite knowledge, understanding, and skill. Instructional sequences can be a helpful tool for creating such assessments. Making sense of formative assessment results (pre- and ongoing), then, asks teachers to analyze what students produce in terms of the KUDs, where students are in an acquisition/meaning-making/transfer loop, where they are working in an instructional sequence—or in light of whatever other patterns help the teacher understand students' current development so that the teacher can plan learning opportunities for students or clusters of students to ensure their continuing academic growth. As Hattie (2012b) states:

> The lesson does not end when the bell goes! It ends when teachers interpret the evidence of their impact on students during the lesson(s) relative to their intended learning intentions and initial criteria of success—that is, when teachers review learning through the eyes of their students. (p. 145)

Clarity about content goals or learning targets (KUDs) and instructional sequences positions a teacher to engage in this kind of analysis of student work and to make adjustments indicated by the patterns they see in the work their students did. The "cases in point" at the end of this chapter illustrate this kind of analysis and instructional modification.

Planning with Student Variance in Mind

The goal of all assessment, and certainly pre- and ongoing assessment, is to elicit the most accurate representation possible of a student's actual knowledge, understanding, and skill. For that reason, it's worth considering whether differentiating the assessment would make it likely that some students would have a better opportunity to demonstrate their learning. As with pre-assessments, ongoing formative assessments can be differentiated in the mode of expression, working conditions, application to particular interests, and so on. What cannot change are the goals (KUDs) the assessment is designed to measure. Given research (e.g., Tomlinson & McTighe, 2006) suggesting that appropriately challenging work, work that addresses student interests, and formats that make work proceed more efficiently enhance student learning, it is again worth reflecting on whether those same conditions would improve assessment outcomes. Although standardized tests are not designed to address variance in readiness, interest, or learning profile, it is wise to remember that the process of assessment should facilitate learning rather than constrict it with the looming presence of a single year-end measure which is likely to produce better results anyhow if the learning process supports students in making maximum progress throughout the year.

Designing and Using Ongoing Assessments: A Quick Review

To promote learning, ongoing assessment requires three elements: (1) clear learning goals, (2) information about the learner relative to those goals, and (3) action to close the gap (National Research Council, 2001). Emphasizing the central purpose of formative assessment in a differentiated classroom, action to close the gap, Earl (2003) asserts:

> Assessment, instead of being the means for categorizing students and avoiding working to help them learn, becomes the mechanism for deciding what to do to push learning forward. . . . Finding out about students as learners and as people is the key to differentiation. When teachers are equipped with detailed knowledge about their students and have a clear idea about what the students need to learn, differentiation can happen all the time. (p. 87)

Ongoing assessment is, of course, also instrumental in determining students who are progressing "on schedule" as well as those who show early mastery of KUDs and therefore need learning opportunities designed to extend their academic growth as well. Simply said, ongoing assessment is key to effective instructional planning for all students.

Figure 4.6 summarizes the purposes of ongoing assessment.

To design formative assessments and use their results to support instructional planning, which is the core purpose of formative assessment, teachers should be able to answer questions such as the following:

- Does the unit have clear KUDs, and are they stated in appropriate form to reflect the nature of the three elements (knowledge, understanding, and skill) and to reflect content standards and the nature of the discipline in which the unit is located?
- What are the KUDs—the essential knowledge, understanding, and skills— that are being checked on this ongoing assessment?

Figure 4.6
The Purposes of Ongoing Assessment

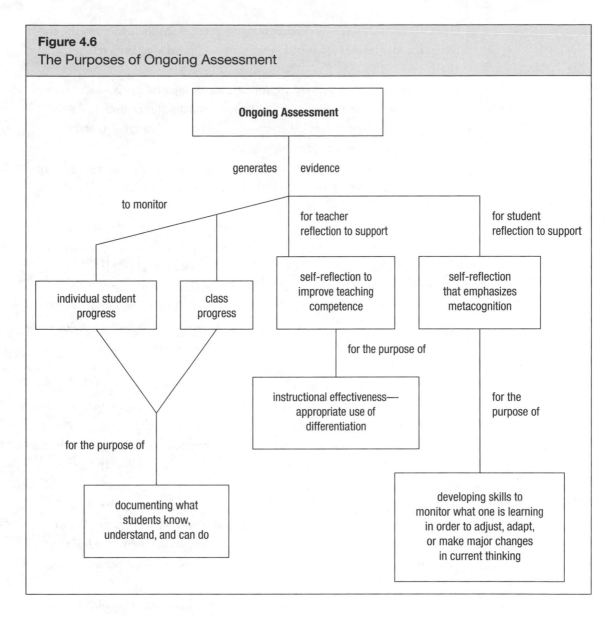

- What prerequisite knowledge, understanding, and skill should be checked at this juncture to ensure that students are ready to move ahead?
- Are there common misunderstandings that should be assessed at this point in the learning cycle?
- Does the assessment measure understanding as well as knowledge and a range of skills? Does it call on students to use the three elements in conjunction with one another?

- Does the assessment reflect instructional sequences that help identify the current status of a learner in a broad progression of knowledge, understanding, or skill?
- Is the format of the assessment appropriate for assessment goals, students being assessed, time available for the assessment, and other contextual needs?
- Are there students who would benefit from differentiation in the way the assessment is written, designed, or administered?
- How will I provide feedback on the formative assessment to students in a way that builds trust and is clear, user-friendly, specific, focused, differentiated, timely, and invites follow-up?
- How might I use the formative assessment information to involve students in a way that helps them develop a growth mind-set, understand the learning process more fully, develop the attitudes and habits of mind that support autonomous learning, and build a sense of classroom community?
- What meaningful differences does the assessment indicate exist among students in the class related to KUDs, learning progressions, an acquisition/sense-making/transfer loop, or other patterns that are useful to informing instruction?
- Based on analysis of meaningful patterns, what does this student or cluster of students need as the unit continues in order to facilitate maximum growth toward the essential goals of the unit, and beyond them when appropriate?
- How does my evolving knowledge of student interests suggest I might help students connect upcoming knowledge, understanding, and skill with their lives, experiences, strengths, and passions?
- Given what I know of students' varied approaches to learning, how might I design upcoming lessons and tasks so that students have opportunities to take in and make sense of what we're learning in ways that make the learning process more inviting and more successful for the broadest possible spectrum of learners?
- In what ways does the assessment information help me reflect on and refine my thinking and instructional planning?

Two Cases in Point

Following are two scenarios of teachers using formative or ongoing assessment in order to know better how to address students' varied readiness levels and interests. The first scenario is drawn from a 3rd grade unit on persuasive writing. The second is a continuation of the market analysis example begun in Chapter 3.

Ongoing Assessment in a 3rd Grade Class

Ms. Beasley's 3rd grade class is working on persuasive writing. It's the first unit students have had on this skill. The unit is based on the following 3rd grade common core writing standards:

- Introduce a topic or text the student is writing about.
- State an opinion and create an organizational structure that lists reasons.
- Provide reasons that support an opinion.
- Use linking words and phrases to connect an opinion and reasons.
- Provide a concluding statement or section.

Ms. Beasley established the following essential question and KUDs for the unit:

Essential Question: How can my writing help people make up their minds?

Know:

- Key vocabulary: *topic sentence, supporting details, elaboration, concluding statement, persuasive paragraph*

- Purpose of a persuasive paragraph

- Parts that make up a persuasive paragraph

Understand:

- The structure of text influences how people make sense of it.

Do:

- Organize an individual paragraph with topic sentence, relevant elaboration, and a concluding sentence.

- Analyze a paragraph to identify key components of a persuasive paragraph.

During the first two language arts blocks in the unit on persuasive writing, Ms. Beasley discussed with students things they'd like people to agree with them about, asked them to share their opinions on several topics 3rd graders usually care about, and read to the class and discussed with them several story excerpts in which characters in stories or writers in other contexts stated their opinions in order to persuade other people to accept their viewpoints. They talked about the word *persuasion,* and Ms. Beasley introduced the class to the elements of a persuasive paragraph. Ms. Beasley underlined in different colors the various elements of a persuasive paragraph on the board and discussed them with the class. Students then worked in pairs to talk about a paragraph she provided, using the vocabulary of persuasive writing.

At that point, Ms. Beasley used the following formative assessment to get a sense of students' understanding of how they could use the elements of persuasion to construct a persuasive paragraph:

> *Read the following prompt and let us know what you think about the issue in it. Use the parts of a persuasive paragraph to help someone know what your point of view is about the decision and why. Remember, your writing can help people make up their minds. Persuade us that you are right.*
>
> The school board met and decided that recess would no longer be needed in school. They felt that it would help students spend more time learning without being interrupted each day for recess. What do YOU think?

After reading the student paragraphs, Ms. Beasley concluded that there were two clusters of students—those who appeared to understand and generally be able to use the key elements of a persuasive paragraph, and those who were not able to do so. For the next lesson, she called the two groups the Quarter Pounder Group and the Big Mac Group and designed the lesson to address their different points of readiness.

At the beginning of the next class, she reintroduced the pre-assessment topic and had the students think-pair-share about their opinions on the topic. She then asked pairs to read two sample paragraphs she provided. Both reflected the same opinion, but one was organized according to the elements of persuasion and one was not. After reading, students talked about which paragraph they felt was more persuasive and why.

Then Ms. Beasley reviewed with the whole group the vocabulary of organizing a persuasive paragraph—*topic sentence, supporting details, elaboration, concluding sentence.* As she reviewed each definition, all students highlighted the example in a model paragraph with markers (green = topic sentence, blue = supporting details, orange = elaborations, red = concluding sentence). Here is the model paragraph:

> There are many reasons why we shouldn't have recess during the school day. First of all, if we didn't have recess, we would have more time to work on projects in school without being interrupted. Sometimes I am in the middle of something really, really important, and then all of a sudden, we have to stop and I have to leave it behind. By not having recess, fewer students would get hurt on the playground. It seems like every time we are out on the playground, someone trips or falls and needs to go to the nurse. Finally, by not having recess, we might do better on tests. Everyone would have longer to study and we could all get As. So you see, if we didn't have recess, it would be good for our school.

Following this whole-class segment, Ms. Beasley put up two large pieces of paper on opposite sides of the room. Each piece contained the names of students in one of the clusters indicated by the formative assessment. Students went to the area where their names were posted and found directions for their next step.

Students in the group that was more proficient with developing a persuasive paragraph found Quarter Pounder boxes from McDonald's along with the following directions:

- Each pair of students should pick up a Quarter Pounder box. With a partner, work on the jumbled paragraph inside the box. When you both feel that it is organized like a good persuasive paragraph, get an answer key and check your work. Correct your paragraph if you need to, glue it to a piece of paper, and turn it in with both partners' names on it.

- Meet with the teacher to talk about a model for persuasive paragraphs. Your teacher will give you a graphic organizer that you can use to organize a persuasive paragraph you will write.

- Complete the following assignment: Choose one of the following topics for a persuasive paragraph and tell us what you think about it so you persuade us you are right. Use the graphic organizer to guide your thinking. Do this part by yourself.

  - Should chewing gum be allowed in class?
  - Should students be allowed to bring toys to school?
  - Do dogs make better pets than cats?

Your paragraph will be reviewed according to how well you organize your ideas using the elements of a persuasive paragraph.

When students in the Quarter Pounder group met with Ms. Beasley, she gave them the graphic organizer in Figure 4.7 and discussed it with them.

In another area of the room, students in the cluster that appeared less certain of how to write a persuasive paragraph found Big Mac boxes from McDonald's along with the following directions:

- Each student should pick up a Big Mac box. Work with a partner to make a good persuasive paragraph from the jumbled strips inside your box. When you both think the paragraph is organized, raise your hands to have the teacher check your answers. Glue your corrected paragraph to a piece of paper and turn it in with your name on it.

- Meet with the teacher to talk about a model for a persuasive paragraph. The teacher will give you a graphic organizer to help you write a good persuasive paragraph.

Figure 4.7
Graphic Organizer for Students Needing Less Help in Writing a Persuasive Paragraph

Topic: _____

By _____

Topic Sentence:

Supporting Detail:

1. Elaboration:
2. Elaboration:

Supporting Detail:

1. Elaboration:
2. Elaboration:

Supporting Detail:

1. Elaboration:
2. Elaboration:

Concluding Statement:

- Complete the following assignment: Choose one of the questions below to be your topic for a persuasive paragraph. Fill out your graphic organizer to be sure your thoughts are organized to include the parts of a persuasive paragraph. Then write your persuasive paragraph using the graphic organizer to guide your writing.
  - Should chewing gum be allowed in class?
  - Should students be allowed to bring toys to school?
  - Do dogs make better pets than cats?

  Your paragraph will be reviewed according to how well you organize your ideas using the elements of a persuasive paragraph.

When students in the Big Mac Group met with Ms. Beasley, she gave them the graphic organizer in Figure 4.8 and discussed it with them. She also discussed with them a completed organizer and showed them a persuasive paragraph written from the organizer. In addition, she pointed them to an Extra Toppings center in the part of the room where they were working and explained how they might use the "extra toppings questions" to think of ideas to support their opinions as they completed the organizer. In the center were "extra toppings jars" for each of the questions from which students could select their topic. Figure 4.9 shows an example of a jar and its questions.

Ms. Beasley gave her students feedback on their paragraphs based on each student's use of the elements of a persuasive paragraph. In addition to brief comments on the papers about each paragraph element, she created a small checklist in grid form (Figure 4.10) that allowed her to mark each element as "used correctly" or "needs work" so that students could easily see how they were doing with each paragraph element. The grid provided space for students to plan for their next steps in writing a persuasive paragraph. The teacher met briefly with each student while the class was working independently at centers or on classwork to discuss the student's plans and to point out both center work and homework that would help the student continue to grow as a writer of persuasive paragraphs.

In the next couple of lessons, Ms. Beasley continued to share examples of persuasive writing with students for class discussion and analysis. The discussions focused on the essential question "How can writing help people make up their minds?" Students discussed the role each element of persuasion played in helping them understand the writers' opinions. Center work included opportunities for students to practice, refine, and extend their skills with each of the elements of persuasion. She met with small groups during the language arts blocks to reteach, clarify, or extend student thinking. She differentiated homework for the students over three nights to allow students to focus on their particular next steps in persuasive writing.

Figure 4.8

Graphic Organizer for Students Needing More Help in Writing a Persuasive Paragraph

Topic: _____

By _____

Topic Sentence: What do I believe about this?
What is my overall opinion about this?

Supporting Detail: What is one reason that I believe what I said in my topic sentence?

1. Elaboration: What is an example of how I know the supporting detail is true?
2. Elaboration: What is another example of how I know the supporting detail is true?

Supporting Detail: What is another reason that I believe what I said in my topic sentence?

1. Elaboration: What is an example of how I know the supporting detail is true?
2. Elaboration: What is another example of how I know the supporting detail is true?

Supporting Detail: What is another reason that I believe what I said in my topic sentence?

1. Elaboration: What is an example of how I know the supporting detail is true?
2. Elaboration: What is another example of how I know the supporting detail is true?

Concluding Statement: How can I let the reader know that I'm finished with giving supporting details? (Hint: Start with, "So . . ." or "Therefore . . ." or "In Summary . . .")

Figure 4.9
Extra Toppings Jar and Questions

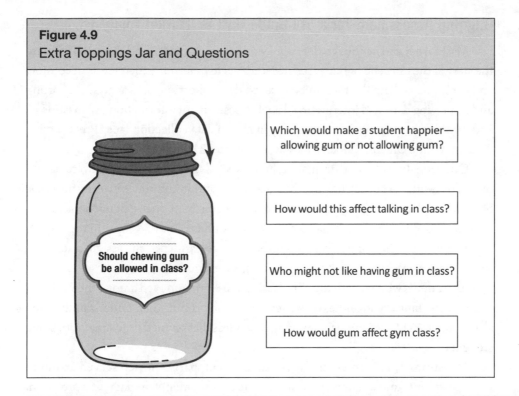

Should chewing gum be allowed in class?

Which would make a student happier—allowing gum or not allowing gum?

How would this affect talking in class?

Who might not like having gum in class?

How would gum affect gym class?

Figure 4.10
Teacher Feedback and Student Planning Grid for Writing Persuasive Paragraphs

Element of Persuasion	Used Correctly	Needs Work	Plan for My Next Step
Topic Sentence			
Supporting Details			
Elaboration			
Concluding Statement			

Ongoing Assessment for a 6th Grade Unit on Market Analysis

Ms. Horner and her 6th graders were working on a unit on market analysis. Before the start of the unit, she pre-assessed her students to determine their levels of comfort and competence with the four unit concepts: data collection, data analysis, reporting and displaying data, and interpreting data. Pre-assessment information on questions 5 and 7 guided her planning for the unit segment on data collection (see "Pre-assessing for a 6th Grade Unit on Market Analysis" in Chapter 3).

Question 4 related to data analysis and revealed that some students were having difficulties with fractions, whereas others appeared more comfortable in using fractions. She gave students an additional, brief formative assessment on use of fractions in data analysis shortly before she began working with students on that topic in the second segment of the unit. Using information from both assessments, she assigned students to a tiered assignment on multiplying fractions (see Figure 4.11).

As students worked with the tiered tasks, Ms. Horner moved among them, checking on their status, taking notes on what she saw, and probing their understanding. She also sometimes offered minilessons on skills or ideas that seemed problematic for some students.

Questions 1, 2, 3, and 6 on the pre-assessment, part of which served an ongoing assessment function as well, related to the unit segments on data interpretation, reporting, and display. Those questions suggested that all students in the class were at a relatively similar level of understanding and skill in those areas. For that reason, she conducted whole-class lessons on data interpretation, reporting, and display, with opportunities for students to work together in interest-based groups to practice and apply what they were learning.

Ms. Horner also worked with the language arts teacher to determine student proficiency in expository writing—an important skill for successful completion of the performance task that would be part of the unit. Based on information provided by the language arts teacher, she conducted small-group minilessons on expository writing focused on the particular readiness needs of three subsets of students and on the skills related to the summative performance task. Figure 4.12 summarizes the sequence of the unit, showing both whole-class and differentiated elements.

The performance assessment for the unit measured students' proficiency with collecting data; calculating fractions, decimals, and percentages based on data; and displaying and reporting data in graphic and written form through a market analysis project. Students took on the role of employees of a market analysis firm that had been hired by a clothing retailer to provide good information on what kinds of shoes to stock for young people. The "employees" designed and conducted a survey of students' shoe preferences, analyzed the survey data, reported findings, and explained the processes they used. The performance assessment was differentiated by readiness with two

Figure 4.11

A Tiered Lesson on Multiplying Fractions Based on Ongoing Assessment

Group 1 On-grade-level readiness in multiplying fractions	**Teacher input:** Problems involve multiplying fractions by multiplying numerators and denominators and reducing the product to simplest form. Students can check their work with fraction strips if needed.	**Student tasks:** • Students complete practice sets on multiplying fractions. The first half of the set requires students to use a new method. In the second half, students have their choice of methods. • Students check their answers with a buddy when finished.
Group 2 Above-grade-level readiness in multiplying fractions	**Teacher input:** Multistep problems require multiplication of fractions (making blueprints to scale). Students first convert data to a common unit (yards, feet, inches), then multiply.	**Student tasks:** • Students complete practice sets on multiplying fractions. Each set of problems asks students to convert data using customary measures of capacity and weight. • Students check their answers with a buddy when finished.
Group 3 Below-grade-level readiness in multiplying fractions	**Teacher input:** Problems use construction-paper fraction strips as a concrete example of multiplying fractions. Teacher demonstrates spatially the relationship of the fractions.	**Student tasks:** • Students complete practice problems on multiplying fractions using fraction strip sets. • Students check their answers with a buddy when finished.

Figure 4.12

Sequence of Instructional Components in Market Analysis Unit

Whole Class	Differentiated
Administer pre-assessment.	
Introduce performance assessment and rubric for end of the unit so students can work with the end in mind.	
Conduct whole-class lessons on sampling.	
Explain contract requirements and working conditions.	Give students blue or yellow contract folders and have them complete contract assignments.
	Conduct minilessons on sampling based on need (pre-assessment).
Conduct whole-class lessons on fractions, whole numbers.	Give independent work to small group of students who have already mastered concepts related to fractions and whole numbers.
	Give tiered assignment on multiplying fractions.
Conduct whole-class lessons on displaying, reporting, and interpreting data.	
Collect writing-levels information and samples from language arts teacher as formative information to form groups for minilessons on writing.	

Whole Class	Differentiated
	Conduct minilessons on expository writing in flexible groups based on student writing strengths and needs.
	Students complete performance task that includes two readiness-based prompts.
Students share their summative performance products with whole class. (All students provide feedback to peers on index cards using pre-established criteria.)	

versions of the prompt. The first version was designed to assess mathematical contexts and processes at approximately grade level. The second was designed for students who were working beyond grade level in mathematical concepts and processes and who also evidenced effective abstract thinking. The second prompt provided students with less structure in choosing characteristics to consider in their research and required them to manipulate more variables than the first version required.

In both examples, the teachers are quite clear about what students should know, understand, and be able to do as a result of instruction. That clarity enables them to create formative assessments that tightly align with their KUDs. In turn, analysis of student work on the formative assessments provides the teachers with focused information about each student's current proficiency with the desired outcomes. This information, in turn, guides the teachers in decision making about points in the upcoming instructional sequence at which whole-class instruction is likely to be useful and points at which differentiation is likely to benefit students more than whole-class approaches.

Reflecting on the work of these two teachers suggests that they are simply following a logical line of planning, thought, and inquiry about student development toward important goals. Their mindful approach to facilitating student growth seems little more than common sense. In fact, that is the case. Rather than simply teaching what "comes next" to all students without regard to how the various students responded to what "came before," these two teachers engaged in a fact-finding mission about students' progress and made modest but meaningful adaptations in upcoming lessons based on what they learned. The two teachers used diagnosis to guide prescription—an idea that's as well founded in teaching as in medicine.

5

Summative Assessment: Measuring Student Learning at Key Points in a Unit

> To measure, or to learn; that is the question.
>
> —Patricia Broadfoot, cited in Lorna Earl, *Assessment as Learning*

A common refrain early in the school year from 10th graders in Mr. Murphy's biology class went something like this: "That guy is crazy. The test he gave us yesterday was on something we hadn't even studied. I don't get how he's allowed to do that." The test in question dealt with kidney structure and function in the kangaroo rat. After describing the animal's environment, which is virtually water-free, he posed the question about how the animal manages to survive in such an environment. The test consisted of three or four approximately page-long segments of information, each followed by three or four questions. At the end, students were asked to give their best explanation of how kangaroo rats survive with almost no water in their environment. Students had been studying and applying the method or process of scientific thinking before the test. The test was structured to provide students with information, ask them to hypothesize using that information, provide additional information, ask them to refine their hypotheses based on the new information, test the new hypothesis, and so on. Because the test did not use the language of the scientific method or refer to it in the directions, students generally thought the test was on kangaroo rats, which hadn't come up at all in class or readings.

When Mr. Murphy returned the test and helped students think about its design, they were typically amazed that it did, in fact, focus directly on what they had "learned." He had asked them to engage in a scientific process of thinking and draw conclusions as a result. Mr. Murphy guided the students in thinking about this test and how it was different from others that were more familiar and predictable for them, and about what kind of learning would be necessary to succeed with this new approach to assessment. More to the point, he helped them throughout the year understand what it meant to learn in a way that made knowledge their own rather than to repeat someone else's information.

As the year went on, students' comments shifted. "You know, if you don't truly understand what's going on in biology, Mr. Murphy's tests are killers; but if you do, they're actually kind of cool." By the end of the year, the general consensus of his students was something like this: "In his class, you learn to think and study in a whole new way. I didn't just memorize stuff. I really get it!"

Mr. Murphy was a master at developing summative assessments that contributed to student growth as learners. Sometimes the assessments were performance-based tests. Sometimes they took the form of student products, such as designing experiments for the space shuttle or creating science modules for younger students studying the same topics as his high schoolers. Always, the assessments required understanding, application, and transfer as well as direct content knowledge. Of course, the way he thought about, planned, and carried out instruction was framed with the same intent. He regularly included students in analyzing their own work according to clear criteria for that work. He raised the bar of student expectations for summative assessments and then coached the students in class sessions throughout the year to reach that bar. His class was transformative, and his use of summative assessments was part of the transformation process.

The Nature of Summative Assessment

Summative assessments are more formal and "official" than pre- and ongoing assessments. They are used largely to assess the outcomes of instruction and may come in the form of midterms, chapter tests, unit tests, final exams, projects, and papers (Airasian, 1997). Whereas experts in measurement caution against grading pre-assessments and formative assessments, summative assessments are intended for grading. To say that grades should come largely, if not solely, from summative assessments does not suggest that student report card grades would come from only one or two tests. It is important for students to have multiple opportunities to demonstrate what they have learned. Summative assessments can and should take place multiple times during a marking period and in multiple forms.

Summative assessments sometimes get a bad rap. As Earl (2003) notes:

This is the kind of assessment that still dominates most classroom assessment activities, especially in secondary schools. . . . Teachers use the tests to assess the quantity and accuracy of student work, and the bulk of teacher effort is taken up in marking and grading. A strong emphasis is placed on comparing students, and feedback to students comes in the form of marks or grades, with little advice for improvement. . . . Typically, they don't give much indication of mastery of particular ideas or concepts because the test content is generally too simplistic to represent the broad range of skills and knowledge that has been covered. But this lack of specificity hasn't presented a problem because the teachers' perceived purpose for the assessment is to produce a rank order of the students and assign a symbol to designate the students' position within the group, whatever group it might be. (pp. 22–23)

In reference to grades, Wiggins (1998) notes that there is really nothing wrong with the symbol we call a grade. Rather, the morass that we think of as grading has occurred because of how we think about and use grades. The same might be said of summative assessments. The bad press they sometimes glean derives not from the idea of measuring student achievement at key points in a learning cycle, but rather from how we have gone about doing that. This chapter focuses on attributes and uses of quality summative assessments in general and as they relate to differentiation in particular.

At some points during a unit of study, it is both necessary and important to formally assess students' levels of achievement relative to a predefined set of learning goals (KUDs). Summative assessment refers to this formal process of assessing students' learning at predetermined points in a learning sequence when students have been presented with new knowledge, ideas, and skills and have had opportunities to practice, make sense of, and come to "own" those elements. Also known as assessment *of* learning because it focuses on measuring the degree to which students have achieved pre-identified learning goals, summative assessment can occur at the end of a unit when all of the learning objectives have been taught, at the end of several lessons that form a subset of meaning in the unit, or even at the end of a single lesson if the lesson objective has been fully met and students have had adequate opportunity to achieve mastery. Using summative assessments at the end of a lesson or set of lessons helps teachers ensure that students have developed the foundation on which subsequent lessons will build. Summative assessment takes its name from its purpose of "summing up" what students have learned at a logical point in time.

Formats for Summative Assessment

Summative assessments can employ a variety of tools and methods for gathering information about student learning, and they can provide information about student achievement at the student, classroom, and in some instances, school level. Here we focus on the student and classroom levels. Although assessments *of* learning serve different purposes than assessments *for* or *as* learning, many of the assessment formats—for example, quizzes, writing prompts, and application tasks—can be used in all three contexts.

Formats most commonly associated with assessment *of* learning fall into two broad categories: (1) traditional paper-and-pencil assessments, or closed tasks, which include multiple-choice, short answer, fill-in-the-blank responses, true/false statements, and interpretive items; and (2) performance-oriented assessments, which include essays, extended projects or products, portfolios, and performance tasks. The types of learning goals and the broad intent of the learning should determine which type of assessment is most appropriate for gathering information to document student mastery. In addition to ensuring alignment between the type of assessment and the nature of the learning goals the assessment will measure, it is also important to ensure that the assessment (1) will effectively measure what is intended to be measured (KUDs); (2) focuses on the most essential (versus more peripheral) knowledge, understanding, and skill; and (3) has a format consistent with the time available for students to complete it. Figure 5.1 provides an overview of the various formats for summative assessments, types of evidence each provides, and the limitations associated with each format.

Indicators of Quality Summative Assessments

The concepts of reliability and validity are critical for quality summative assessments. *Reliability* refers to the stability of a measure in obtaining the same results over time or in varied settings. *Validity* refers to the degree of confidence that an assessment actually measures what it is intended to measure. These two concepts are discussed in greater detail in Chapter 6 as they relate to grading. Beyond the baseline requirement that summative assessments should reflect reliability and validity, five additional indicators of quality in summative assessments are discussed in the following text. Many of them should sound familiar, or at least relevant to pre- and ongoing assessment as well, given that quality in pre-assessments, ongoing assessments, and summative assessments are necessarily related.

   Indicator 1: The assessment mirrors the learning goals. As we've established, learning goals, or KUDs, are statements that reflect what students will learn as a result of instruction. Therefore, direct alignment between the goals and the assessment items or tasks used to document the degree to which a student has achieved them is of primary importance. The assessment items or tasks should result in student responses that will appropriately measure that student's proficiency with the knowledge, understanding, and skill designated as critical for the segment of learning targeted by the summative assessment.

   Indicator 2: The content of the assessment reflects the relative importance of each learning goal. The assessment should emphasize the knowledge, understanding, and skill that are most important for the student to master in order to develop competence in the discipline being taught and assessed. Any KUDs that are developed before the start of

Figure 5.1
Types of Summative Assessment

Traditional Paper-and-Pencil (Closed Tasks)
Item Types:

- True/false questions, multiple-choice questions, fill-in-the-blank, matching, solving problems (e.g., mathematics)

Resulting Evidence:

- Can assess simple recall of knowledge to more complex levels of thinking (if constructed appropriately), including discriminating between fact and fiction, interpretation of charts and graphs, making inferences from a given dataset, interpretation of cause-and-effect relationships

Limitations:

- Cannot assess student ability to produce original ideas, provide examples, furnish information, articulate explanations
- Does not assess process skills
- Difficult to create high-quality questions

Performance-Oriented (Performance Tasks)
Item Types:

- Oral presentations, lab demonstrations, debates, musical and dance recitals, athletic competitions, etc.

Resulting Evidence:

- Useful for assessing student ability to organize, synthesize, and apply information
- Useful for assessing process skills
- Useful for assessing student ability to transfer knowledge to other disciplinary domains
- Can be multidisciplinary
- Can measure complex learning outcomes
- Emphasizes integration of thinking and problem solving

Limitations:

- Difficult to create high-quality, relevant tasks
- Can be time-consuming to score
- Provides only a limited sampling of a content area

Performance-Oriented (Constructed Response)
Item Types:

- Constructed responses to posed questions; visual representations such as concept maps, flowcharts, graphic organizers, tables

Resulting Evidence:

- Useful for assessing student use of processes or strategies, application of information, ability to interpret

Limitations:

- Difficult to create high-quality, relevant questions
- Can be time-consuming to score
- Provides only limited sampling of a content area

Performance-Oriented (Products)
Item Types:

- Essays, research papers, lab reports, portfolios, writing projects, science projects, art exhibits

Resulting Evidence:

- Can measure complex learning outcomes
- Emphasizes integration of thinking and problem solving
- Focuses on evaluating the outcome of a process
- Useful for assessing student ability to organize, synthesize, and apply information
- Useful for assessing student ability to transfer knowledge to other disciplinary domains
- Can be multidisciplinary

Limitations:

- Difficult to create high-quality, relevant tasks
- Can be time-consuming to score
- Requires deep understanding of quality scoring rubrics

instruction should make clear what matters most. Instruction should align tightly with the KUDs and therefore emphasize what is most important for students to learn. A summative assessment, then, should measure what was delineated as most essential in the KUDs and in the classroom. If in a particular math unit, for example, it's more important that students be able to represent mathematical relations with equations and less important that they determine a missing term in a sequence, then both classroom instruction and the assessment should reflect this emphasis. Using the process of backward design, curriculum developers begin with statements of essential knowledge, understanding, and skill, then move to developing summative assessments that align with the content goal statements, and finally teach with the intent to ensure that students develop the necessary competencies to succeed on the already developed summative assessments (Wiggins & McTighe, 1998). Careful use of backward design greatly enhances the likelihood of alignment between KUDs, summative assessments, and instruction—and prospects for student success.

Indicator 3: The format of the assessment is aligned with the cognitive level of the learning goals. "To ensure accurate assessment results, the overriding criterion for selection of method is consideration of the type of learning targets to be assessed" (Chappius et al., 2012, p. 87). In other words, the cognitive demands required to respond to the assessment should match the cognitive demands required to master the particular content goals. For example, if the learning goal is simply for students to recall information (that is, repeat facts and definitions, or apply a simple algorithm or formula), then the assessment should only require this level of cognitive demand. In this instance, a multiple-choice or short-answer type of format is often well suited for the relatively low level of cognitive demand required for those goals. If, on the other hand, a learning goal requires students to reason, plan, and use evidence, defend a position, examine varied points of view, and so on, the most appropriate assessment format would be performance oriented—that is, it would have more than one possible answer, require justification of the response, drawing conclusions, combining skills, and so on. In short, the nature of the learning goal should dictate the format of the assessment. Sadly, because it is easier to develop assessments with low cognitive demand, it's common for teachers to say they value student thinking and transfer of ideas to novel situations and then generate assessments that call on students only to repeat what they have heard in class. When summative assessments are low level, the message to students is that real learning is about duplicating someone else's information.

Indicator 4: The range of knowledge indicated by the learning goals is the range of knowledge reflected in instruction, which, in turn, is the range of knowledge needed to appropriately respond to assessment items. Misalignment between specified learning targets and instruction undermines the documentation of learning, even if the assessment is aligned with the learning goals. For example, if a learning goal is to develop students' ability to compare and critique arguments but classroom instruction focuses largely on summarizing arguments and the mechanics of writing, then even though the assessment is designed to measure the stated learning goal, most students will fare poorly because they didn't have the opportunity to practice the skills necessary to succeed on the assessment.

Indicator 5: An assessment should not require students to have specialized knowledge, understanding, skill, or resources beyond what is targeted by the learning goals and is taught or available in class. Today's classrooms are becoming increasingly diverse in terms of language, culture, readiness, economic background, home support system, and other factors. Teachers who are effective for all of their students are aware of these differences in their daily interactions with and instructional planning for their students, and in their assessment practices as well. For assessments to reflect accurately a student's status with specified KUDs, a teacher must consider ways in which students' varied experiential backgrounds might affect their responses to an assessment item and eliminate items or tasks that are outside the context and learning opportunity of some of their students. It's also important in performance-based tasks that may include work time at home that the task not call for resources and support systems that are available to some students outside school but not to others. "Construct irrelevance" causes some students to fare poorly on an assessment not because they don't understand the stated learning goals, but because the assessment requires them to know or do something beyond the scope of their experience. For example, a learning goal and related instruction focuses on the elements of persuasion. A student who currently has a low level of English proficiency and understands the elements of persuasive writing but has not yet developed the skills of written English cannot demonstrate that understanding if she is asked to write a formal, persuasive letter as an indicator of her understanding. "Construct irrelevance" can affect assessment results for students with various handicapping conditions, learning disabilities, cultural backgrounds, experiential levels, and so on, and teachers need to guard against it. In the example of writing a persuasive letter, the student might be allowed to write the letter in his first language and then work with someone to translate it into English.

Summative Assessment and Student Variance: Three Principles

If a teacher differentiates instruction to provide learning opportunities that enable each student to progress as far and as fast as possible, it makes sense that she might elect to consider student differences when designing assessments in order to allow students to demonstrate as fully as possible what they know, understand, and can do as a result. Planning for differentiated summative assessment simply picks up where differentiated instruction left off by asking the following question: "What needs do my students have that I can address in crafting this summative assessment so that they are most likely to be fully able to demonstrate their current points of knowledge, understanding, and skill?" The following three principles should guide teacher construction of differentiated summative assessments.

Principle 1: Differentiated assessments should focus all students on the same essential learning goals (KUDs), with the exception, again, of students whose individualized education plans indicate alternative goals. This principle should be familiar by now. Differentiation is not a plan to provide students with different learning objectives, but rather provides various routes to accomplishing the same essential goals. Summative assessments may be differentiated if a teacher feels that would increase the opportunity students have to reveal what they know, understand, and can do. The differentiation may allow students to apply content goals to one of several interest areas, express themselves in different modes, use different materials, work with directions written at various levels of complexity, and so on. What does *not* change in a differentiated summative assessment is the set of learning outcomes students will be asked to demonstrate.

Principle 2: Students should be assessed in ways that allow them ample opportunity to demonstrate their knowledge, understanding, and skills. This principle encourages teacher flexibility in the assessment design to enable students to have a sound opportunity to demonstrate their learning. Differentiated summative assessments might address student readiness, for instance, by allowing some students to record rather than write their answers, use large-print versions of the assessment, draw and then annotate their ideas rather than using only extended prose, work with a problem that is appropriately challenging, have test items read to them, or have more time to complete the assessment. Likewise, differentiated summative assessments might address student interests by stating a math problem in relation to four interest areas such as music, sports, the stock market, or animals and allowing the student to select which to solve; or inviting students to compare and contrast an author's use of the elements of fiction in a novel they find particularly appealing. Student learning preferences might be addressed by enabling students to demonstrate opposing views of a political issue by writing two letters to the editor or blog entries from individuals with contrasting views or by drawing a series of political cartoons that represent opposing views. Although differentiating summative assessments is not necessary, doing so can yield significant benefits in terms of student opportunity to express learning—as long as the same KUDs are the focus of varied versions of the assessment. Predictably, some teachers will respond by saying, "But the year-end standardized test doesn't address student differences." It's worth considering the likelihood that the more positive and productive a student's learning experiences are up to the moment of that test, the higher the student's level of confidence and competence will be in the high-stakes setting. In fact, research suggests that students tend to perform better on standardized tests when they have had opportunities to learn and express learning in preferred modes, even when the high-stakes test is not in their preferred mode (Sternberg, Torff, & Grigorenko, 1998). There's probably some common sense as well as research behind differentiating summative assessments when warranted.

Principle 3: The scoring system used for evaluating differentiated assessments should be the same regardless of the type of differentiation. What's important in any form of differentiation of assessments is that the learning goals (Principle 1) and the criteria used to evaluate the learning goal (Principle 3) remain the same across all forms (Principle 2). For example, an assessment asks students to propose a healthy diet for three people using the full range of food groups based on the individuals' lifestyles and health needs. In addition to proposing the three diets, students must explain or defend their choices using the unit's key principles or understandings and specific information about the role each food group plays in health. Some students develop charts with their recommendations and explanations, some develop personalized diet notebooks for the individuals, and some role-play conversations between a dietician (themselves) and the three individuals. In every case, student responses should be assessed on whether the student proposed healthy diets for the three individuals, the degree to which the diet was appropriate for the individuals' particular lifestyles, and whether the student effectively used the unit's key principles and sound information about the role of the food groups in health. Unless a learning goal includes doing an effective role-play or making a professional-looking chart, those attributes should not figure in the students' grades. Chapter 6 discusses the idea of 3-P grading, or reporting on student performance (achievement), process (habits of mind and work), and progress (growth in regard to KUDs over time). It is important to encourage students to develop high-quality products—including quality expression and presentation. In that regard, it may be useful to provide students with, or have them develop, criteria for formats in which they elect to work and to provide feedback on those criteria. However, if that feedback converts to a grade, it should be included in a grade for "process" or habits of mind because it relates more to student pursuit of quality than to specified achievement outcomes, and not "averaged in" to a performance grade, which should speak solely to the student's status with the KUDs. In other words, a student should not receive a higher grade on a summative assessment because his monologue was unusually clever or because the cover to his paper was particularly creative (nor should he receive a lower grade because the work wasn't as clever or creative) unless demonstrating cleverness or creativity is a skill noted in the KUDs.

Applying the Principles to Traditional Paper-and-Pencil Assessments

For a classroom teacher, it is often impractical to consider developing differentiated, traditional paper-and-pencil, closed-ended assessments simply because of the complexity of developing alternative items measuring the same content when multiple items are involved. Therefore, it's best to use these closed-ended assessment items only when the identified learning outcomes focus on factual knowledge, concrete reasoning, and discrete, familiar application skills. Even then, however, ways in which students respond to the assessment items and ways in which the items are presented to students can be differentiated (for example, paper-and-pencil versus audio-recorded, read by the student or to the student, response in the first language of an English learner followed by translation versus response in English). It's also possible that specialists in working with students who have identified learning problems might be able to partner with teachers to develop alternate forms of the same closed-ended assessment, ensuring tight alignment to the content goals on the alternate version.

In some instances, however, the nature of the learning goal makes altering some aspects of the assessment inappropriate. For example, if the learning goal states that students will analyze a question of contemporary significance by constructing a formal essay, it would violate the intent of the goal to allow students the option of presenting the analysis in the form of storyboards or political cartoons. Even then, some professional judgment makes sense in regard to students with specific and significant learning challenges—for example, those with a broken writing hand or with diagnosed dysgraphia, or those who are blind or who speak and write very little English. These students might well be able to analyze a question of contemporary significance even if they can't draft an essay in a 40-minute class period using paper and pencil. Students whose learning needs include extended work time might, similarly, demonstrate mastery of the content goals if the time constraints were adjusted. It makes sense to open the way for such students to demonstrate what they do know rather than muting that knowledge because they are unable to meet part of the requirement.

If, on the other hand, the learning goal calls for students simply to analyze a question of contemporary significance, then the form in which students provide a response is not part of the assessment domain (Principle 2). In this instance, allowing students to audio-record a response, prepare and deliver an oral presentation, or create a graphic novel, among other options, would all be acceptable forms of differentiation because there is a "communication" domain that is consistent across the various forms of response (Principle 3). Regardless of the response format, students will be assessed on the degree to which ideas are expressed clearly and effectively. Criteria for all formats could include elements such as organization of ideas, use of resources to develop ideas, clarity of expression, mechanics of expression, or other skills specified in the KUDs.

Applying the Principles to Performance-Oriented Assessments

Summative assessments that are performance oriented (performance tasks, constructed response, products) almost inevitably include room for differentiation in response to student readiness, interest, and learning profile. Following this section are three "cases in point" that illustrate principles of effective use of summative assessment. Scenario 1 is drawn from a differentiated authentic assessment in the content areas of secondary-level social studies and language arts; it illustrates the opportunity for such assessments to adjust for student variance while maintaining constancy with learning goals. In this example, students have the choice of concentrating their work in three of the following areas based on their interests: art, civil rights, economics, military conflicts, technology, or politics. They also have the option of developing an essay or a monologue for their response, reflecting differentiation based on learning preference or learning profile. Finally, differentiation for readiness occurs in two key ways. First, students may draw from a broad range of resources for their work, enabling them to use materials at appropriate readability levels. They can work with the media specialist and teacher to find appropriately challenging resources. In addition, advanced students are challenged to look at the assignment from dual perspectives rather than selecting a single perspective for their work. Regardless of the areas of interest, the mode of presentation, or the readiness adaptations, all responses are assessed in the domain areas of historical accuracy, perspective, persuasiveness, thoroughness, and reference/research skills, and all students focus on the same learning goals.

It would also be appropriate to differentiate this assessment based on students' varied readiness needs in other ways. For example, the teacher might assist students who have difficulty with task management by having them establish daily goals toward the completion of the summative task. Once again, the differentiation does not change the learning goals around which student responses must be constructed, but rather provides scaffolding to eliminate the barriers to students demonstrating their proficiency or to extend the challenge level with the identified learning goals.

Designing and Using Summative Assessments: A Quick Review

Summative assessment or assessment *of* instruction has the purpose of evaluating and grading student proficiency with specified content goals (KUDs) after students have had opportunity to learn about and practice the content goals. Figure 5.2 summarizes the purposes of summative assessment.

Summative assessments can and should take place several times, at summing-up points during a unit of study. Summative assessments typically fall into one of two broad categories: (1) traditional paper-and-pencil assessments such as multiple-choice and fill-in-the-blank tests, and (2) performance-oriented assessments such as authentic assessments, performance-based tasks, and student products or projects. Assessments in the former category are generally better suited for assessing student knowledge and reproduction-level skills, although they can be developed to assess more complex knowledge and skills as well. The latter category is generally more appropriate for assessing student proficiency with complex thinking, application and transfer of knowledge, and "real" (versus schoolhouse) problem solving. The goals or purpose of an assessment should direct a teacher's choice about its format.

Quality summative assessments have the following attributes. They

- Are aligned very tightly with KUDs (content goals) as stated and as taught.
- Focus on the most essential knowledge, understanding, and skill (versus more tangential or peripheral examples).
- Are aligned with the cognitive levels of the learning goals.
- Do not require that students have specialized knowledge or materials and support systems beyond those available in class.

When summative assessments are differentiated, the various versions should

- Keep the KUDs constant for all versions.
- Be designed to open up the assessment process so that all students have a chance to demonstrate their knowledge, understanding, and skill.
- Use the same scoring system regardless of the type of differentiation.

Three Cases in Point

This section contains three examples of differentiated summative performance tasks. The first is a performance-based task for a middle school social studies unit and integrates some content goals from language arts as well. Students prepared the task over an extended period, working both in and out of class. The second task is also a middle school performance-based task and comes at the end of a study on experimental design in science. Students completed this task in a specified time period during class, followed by a class discussion of their ideas and work. The third example is a summative product or project assignment from a 2nd grade science study of pets. The unit helps students see relationships between people's pets and other animals they studied earlier in science. The product also calls on students to use some key language arts competencies. Each example concludes with a brief explanation of how the summative assessment was differentiated.

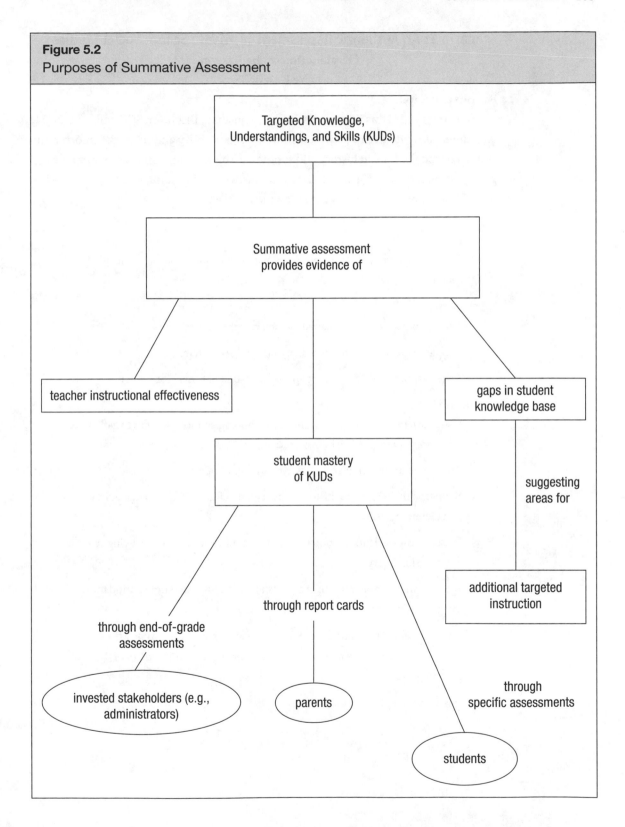

Figure 5.2
Purposes of Summative Assessment

Scenario 1: An Authentic Assessment in Middle School Social Studies
(Explanation of the Assessment)
The Best of Times

Purpose/Rationale

The purpose of this assessment (Moon, Callahan, Brighton, & Tomlinson, 2002) is to determine the extent to which students can identify and interpret information about a particular time in history and synthesize this information into a written or oral presentation reflecting the point of view of someone living at that time.

The assessment addresses the following KUDs:

Know:

- Key vocabulary: *voice, tone, perspective, nationalism, race, religion, ethnicity, synthesize*

Understand:

- People's perspectives are shaped by their circumstances.

- People shape their culture and their culture shapes them.

- "The best of times" for some people is "the worst of times" for others.

Be able to do:

- Use a variety of information-gathering technologies and resources to gather accurate information that will inform student thinking and expression.

- Synthesize information and ideas from multiple sources.

- Support a main idea with historically accurate references to actual people, events, and technologies.

- Present historical information from the point of view of someone living at a specified time in history.

- Address and represent multiple aspects of life in a specified time period in an integrated and accurate way.

- Use vocabulary, tone, costume, or other devices or artifacts to typify the time period being presented in a way that enhances the authenticity of the presentation.

- Report sources in a standard format.

Related Standards

History/Social Studies

The student will develop skills for historical analysis, including the ability to ...

- Identify, analyze, and interpret primary sources and contemporary media and to make generalizations about events and lifestyles in the United States since 1877.

- Recognize and explain how different points of view have been influenced by nationalism, race, religion, and ethnicity.

English

The student will write narratives, descriptions, and explanations:

- Establish central idea, organization, elaboration, and unity.

- Select vocabulary and information to enhance the central idea, tone, and voice.

The student will use writing as a tool for learning in all subjects:

- Synthesize information to construct new concepts.

(Student Assignment)
The Best of Times?

Throughout history, progress (social, technological, artistic, etc.) has led some people to believe that the time in which they are living is, in many ways, "the best of times," whereas others see the time period as "the worst of times." Travel back in time to a particular year. (Your teacher will give you the appropriate date.) Who might you be?

Develop a role for yourself. Are you male or female? How old are you? What race are you? What are your ethnic origins? Where do you live? How long has your family lived in this region? Are you employed? What is your occupation? If you are a kid, what are your aspirations? What do you want to do when you grow up?

Think about ways your life is better than it was for people like you in years past—or ways in which your life is worse than it was for people like you in years past.

From the perspective of your new role, write an essay or develop a monologue to be presented to the class designed to convince others that, for you, these are the best of times or the worst of times. In doing this, describe your life relative to *at least three* of the following areas:

- Art (including drama, dance, music, etc.)
- Civil rights/social movements
- Economic circumstances

- Military conflicts
- New inventions/technology
- Politics

In collecting information for this project, you may use any electronic or print material you like, but you should go beyond our textbook and draw generously from primary sources. Please prepare a written reference list detailing the sources of your information and how you located them.

Evaluation Criteria

Your project will be evaluated according to the following criteria:

- Historical accuracy—How accurate are your facts and other information about the time period?
- Perspective/point of view—How "true" are you to your role? Do the opinions you present correspond with the life and lifestyle of the individual you are portraying?
- Persuasiveness—Does the reader/listener believe that you are from this time period? Are your arguments convincing about why this is the worst or best of times for you?
- Thoroughness—To what extent have you addressed three of the major areas listed (arts, civil rights, economic circumstances, etc.) and shown how those elements shape your perspective about the quality of life you are experiencing?
- Research skills—To what extent did you use a variety of information-gathering techniques? Do you use both primary and secondary resources? Do you effectively synthesize ideas and information from multiple sources?
- Reference skills—To what extent do you report your sources in a standardized format?

A copy of the evaluation form for your work is attached.

The Best of Times Scoring Rubric

Criteria	Exceeds Expectations	Meets Expectations	Is Below Expectations
Historical Accuracy Score: _____	References to actual people, events, technologies, etc., are appropriate to the time period and sufficiently detailed to place them accurately.	References to actual people, events, technologies, etc., are appropriate to the time period, with the exception of minor errors that do not distort the overall feel for the time period.	References to actual people, events, technologies, etc., are inaccurate, incomplete, or inconsistent with the time period.
Perspective/ Point of View Score: _____	Views and opinions expressed consistently reflect both the time period and the character's circumstances.	Views and opinions expressed are appropriate to the time period and the character's circumstances. Minor inconsistencies do not detract from the overall effect.	There are inconsistencies between the views and opinions expressed and the character's time period or circumstances.
Persuasiveness Score: _____	Multiple methods (vocabulary, tone, costume, etc.) are effectively used to convince the reader/audience of the character's authenticity.	More than one method (vocabulary, tone, costume, etc.) is used to persuade the reader/audience that the individual is from the target time period.	Little or no effort is made to persuade the reader/audience that the character is from the time period portrayed.
Thoroughness Score: _____	The unit's three essential understandings are very clearly communicated and supported by a broad range of details in three or more of the following areas: art, civil rights/social movements, economic circumstances, military conflicts, new inventions/technology, and politics.	The unit's three essential understandings are accurately communicated and supported with some detail in three of the following areas: art, civil rights/social movements, economic circumstances, military conflicts, new inventions/technology, and politics.	The unit's three essential understandings are not clearly communicated, or are supported by detail in only one or two of the following areas: art, civil rights/social movements, economic circumstances, military conflicts, new inventions/technology, and politics; or detail is lacking.
Research Skills Score: _____	Resources are appropriate to the task. Multiple primary and secondary resources beyond the textbook are consulted or unique information-gathering techniques are used. Resources used are mainly primary sources. Information is synthesized effectively from resources.	Resources are appropriate to the task. Information gathering extends beyond the textbook but relies mainly on secondary sources. Information is not always well synthesized.	Information gathering is limited to the textbook, or resources used are inappropriate to the task. Information is often not synthesized, making it sound like "copy and paste" from multiple resources rather than ideas blended from multiple resources.
Reference Skills Score: _____	Sources are referenced in a standard, professional format.	Sources are referenced, but not always in a standard, professional format.	Sources are not referenced.

Comments:

Differentiation in Scenario 1

This performance task was differentiated three ways. Readiness differentiation included use of resources at a broad range of readability levels and assistance from the teacher and media specialist in finding and selecting resources at an appropriate readability level for each student. Some resources were also available in languages other than English for English language learners. Assistance with translation of materials from English or students' writing from their first language to English was available through an ELL specialist. In addition, students working at advanced levels with reading, expression, and critical thinking were asked to look at ways in which the three elements they selected had the potential to make the time period both the "best of times" and the "worst of times" for them, their family, and close friends and associates. The minor change in directions required students to consider at least two perspectives on ways in which the selected elements might affect people "like them" during the specified time period, thus requiring more complex thinking. Differentiation in interest occurred as students selected three elements from a longer list of cultural elements as the focus of their work. Students also had the learning-profile option of expressing their work in writing or orally.

Scenario 2: A Constructed-Response Assessment in Middle School Science

(Explanation of the Assessment)
Excellent Experiment or Sloppy Science?

Purpose/Rationale

This assessment (Moon et al., 2002) provides students with an opportunity to demonstrate their understanding of the parts of an experiment. It has been designed to measure students' early understanding of single-variable experimental design and to foster discussion about variables. Presented with a description of research conducted by a younger student, middle school students are asked to evaluate the younger student's work.

The assessment addresses the following KUDs:

Know:

- Key vocabulary: *experiment, research question, independent variable, dependent variable, repeated measures, constants, trial, conclusion*

Understand:

- Each part of a scientific experiment plays an important role in creating accurate and trustworthy conclusions.

- Improper use of any part of a scientific experiment increases the likelihood of experimental error.

Be able to do:

- Evaluate a simple scientific investigation, in particular the appropriateness of research questions, independent and dependent variables, constants, number of trials performed, and conclusions.

- Interpret data tables.

- Interpret SI (metric) units correctly.

- Identify sources of experimental error.

- Effectively express evaluation conclusions in letter format, using appropriate elaboration to support those conclusions.

- Communicate effectively and listen respectfully in a class discussion.

Related Standards

Students will . . .

- Plan and conduct investigations.

- Correctly interpret data organized into tables and showing repeated trials and means.

- Define variables correctly.

- Use or interpret SI (metric) units correctly.

- Establish criteria for making a prediction.

- Identify sources of experimental error.

- Identify dependent variables, independent variables, and constants.

- Demonstrate understanding of why variables are controlled to test hypotheses and why trials are repeated.

- Evaluate or defend varied interpretations of the same set of data.

- Give and seek information in conversations and in group discussions.

- Develop expository writing, elaborating on a central idea in an organized manner.

Evaluation Criteria

- Review of research and related justifications

- Written communication of ideas

- Contributions to group discussion

(Student Assignment)
Excellent Experiment or Sloppy Science?

You are an assistant editor of a new science magazine written for kids, by kids. One of your responsibilities is to review submitted articles and decide whether or not they are suitable for publication. Jeffrey Davis, a 5th grade student from Indiana, has submitted an article describing an experiment he conducted to find out whether putting worms in the soil of house plants would make the plants grow better. Your job is to do the following:

1. Read the attached article and decide whether you wish to include it in the magazine.
2. Write a letter to Jeffrey, explaining your decision based on his use of the parts of an experiment.

Your decision will be one of the following:

A. The experiment sounds well designed and executed, and the article will appear in the next issue of the magazine. (Describe the strengths of the experiment.)
B. The experiment is a good idea, but it has some problems. Jeffrey may resubmit the article with appropriate modifications. (Explain the changes he must make and why you think they are important.)
C. The experiment has many flaws. You are unable to include the article in the magazine. (Describe the problems.)

Because this is your first day on the job, your boss will supervise your work. She will be checking to make sure that you reviewed the major components of Jeffrey's experiment, and that you have explained any problems you discovered. An Experiment Review Form has been included to help you with this. You must turn in both the review form and your letter, and you are expected to share your findings in a discussion with the other assistant editors.

Assignment Summary
- Read "Worms Are Winners" by Jeffrey Davis.
- Complete the Experiment Review Form.
- Write a short letter to Jeffrey explaining your decision regarding his article.
- Participate in a discussion of Jeffrey's work and the reasons for your decision about its publication.

Your boss will use the attached Performance Assessment Form to review *your* work.

Worms Are Winners

by Jeffrey Davis

Worms are winners! They help your plants grow. I thought that they would, so I did an experiment. My research question was this: What is the effect of earthworms on plant growth? I dug up some worms from one of the gardens at my school, and I put them in the soil of some of our houseplants at home. I added one worm to an African violet, two worms to a fern, and three worms to a spider plant. For my control plant I used a cactus and didn't add any worms. I put all the plants on the same window sill so that they would get the same amount of light, and I gave them the same amount of water each week when I measured their height. My results can be seen in the graph below.

As you can see in the graph, the cactus (no worms) did not grow at all. The spider plant (three worms) grew the most. The violet (one worm) did not grow as much as the fern (two worms). Therefore, you should add worms to the soil of your houseplants—the more the better.

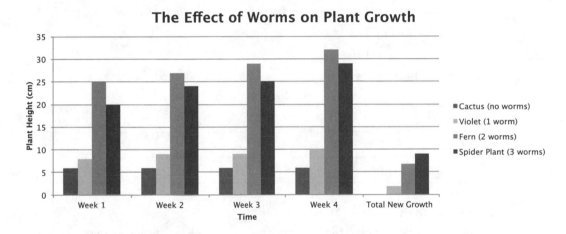

The Effect of Worms on Plant Growth

Experiment Review Form

Research Question

Does the author clearly state the question he or she is trying to answer?

_____ YES: The research question is_____

_____ NO: Recommendations:

Independent Variable

Does the author identify a single independent variable to be manipulated?

_____ YES: The independent variable is _____

_____ NO: Recommendations:

Dependent Variable

Does the author identify the dependent variable to be measured?

_____ YES: The dependent variable is _____

_____ NO: Recommendations:

Constants

Does the author keep all variables that are under his or her control constant, EXCEPT the independent variable?

_____ YES   _____ NO

Variables held constant: Variables not held constant:

_____   _____

_____   _____

_____   _____

_____   _____

Number of Trials

Does the author use enough trials to convince you that the results are not due to chance?

_____ YES   Number of Trials: _____

_____ NO   Recommendations:

Conclusions

What conclusion does the author draw from the experimental results?
Is the author's conclusion supported by the experimental results?

_____ YES, the author's conclusion is supported by the experimental results.

_____ NO, there may be other explanations for the results, such as the following:

_____

Performance Assessment Form

Associate Editor _____

Differentiation in Scenario 2

Criteria	Powerfully Proficient (3 points)	Quite Competent (2 points)	Rethinking Required (1 point)
Review of Research Score: _____	Excellent job reviewing Jeffrey's article. You identified at least three significant problems with Jeffrey's research and provided detailed explanations of these errors.	Good job reviewing Jeffrey's article. You identified at least two significant problems with Jeffrey's research and provided an explanation of your critique.	You need to be more careful in your review. You overlooked major mistakes in Jeffrey's research. You were not thorough in your explanations of his errors.
Written Communication of Ideas Score: _____	Excellent job on your letter to Jeffrey. You defended your decision whether or not to publish his article by clearly explaining in detail both the strong and weak areas of his experiment, as well as your suggestions for improvement. You were well organized, polite, and projected an air of professionalism.	Good job on your letter to Jeffrey. You explained your decision whether or not to publish his article and suggested ways he could improve his experiment. Your writing was well organized.	Your letter to Jeffrey needs improvement. Your writing was disorganized. You did not explain your decision about publishing his article or offer suggestions for improvement. Your writing was hard to follow.
Contributions to Group Discussion Score: _____	Excellent job contributing to the discussion of Jeffrey's article. You shared some important points about his experiment, and you listened and responded respectfully and thoughtfully to the ideas of others.	Good job contributing to our discussion of Jeffrey's article. You shared some valuable ideas. You were a respectful listener.	Your group discussion skills need improvement. You did not share your ideas. You were not respectful of the ideas of others or did not listen well to their ideas.

This example does not contain differentiation for student interest or learning profile. Readiness differentiation occurred in two ways. First, there was support for students learning English and students who struggle with written expression; English language learners had the option of writing their response in their first language and translating (or working with a translator when available) later. Second, students who have difficulty organizing ideas or who may have difficulty recalling the elements of an experiment received the Experiment Review Form as an organizer to guide their work. Other students simply wrote the required letter to Jeffrey. Their directions did not mention the Experiment Review Form, but rather asked them to explain to Jeffrey the degree to which he had appropriately used each element of experimental design in his work, and to use illustrations from Jeffrey's paper and graph to support their thinking.

Scenario 3: A 2nd Grade Summative Product in Science
(Explanation of the Assessment)
Pets R Us

Purpose/Rationale

This summative assessment occurred near the end of the school year in a 2nd grade classroom. The focus of student work is a continuing study of animals, this time with an emphasis on pets. The teacher wants students to connect what they have been learning about other animals to pets they have or would like to have someday. Several language arts goals are also integrated into the assessment work. The assessment consists of two key parts. First, students work together to create a magazine on pets that they will share with other students in their school (1st, 2nd, and 3rd graders). In addition, students present their work to an audience of parents, school administrators, and faculty to explain how their work represents the "big ideas" about animals and the skills they have been working on. The project lasted for about six weeks, using some (but not all) of the time available in both science and language arts blocks during that period.

The teacher shared copies of several children's magazines with the class on multiple occasions during the year. Students talked about features in the magazines, how the articles were written, who the audiences were, how writers got information for the articles, what editors and artists contributed to the magazines, and so on. As Pets R Us began, she brought the magazines back to the classroom and encouraged students to select a magazine they liked and an article or feature they liked and asked them to share with the class the reasons for their selections. She told the students that they would become magazine publishers over the next few weeks, publishing a magazine about pets for 1st, 2nd, and 3rd graders in their school. She would serve as the editor and students as magazine staff. Students selected a pet about which they would become an expert for the magazine. The pet could be one they currently had, one they used to have, or one they would like to have someday.

Students worked together to decide about things such as the magazine's name, how to best spend their printing budget, and establishing due dates for assignments. Each student created three pieces for the magazine. The first was a comparison between the student's pet and an animal in the wild from the same animal family. The teacher gave students a template for this assignment so that all students would be involved in the same comparison of attributes between a pet and its counterpart in the wild. Second, all students selected a special-interest topic for the magazine—for example, an ad for a pet product, a funny story about a pet, a graph that compares pets in some way, pet trivia, great pet photos with captions, a review of a movie or video about a pet, drawings or paintings of pets, or a cartoon about pets. It was required that all feature articles be authentic, help the audience understand and appreciate the pet better, and use the class "careful writer rules." Third, the teacher assigned each student a feature story for the magazine based on the student's interests and current language skills. Topics included guidelines for caring for one kind of pet, reminders about how pets help people and people help pets, hints about training a kind of pet, animals that make bad pets and why, unusual pets people have in other countries, pets of adults in the school, how pets help people with disabilities, families that train seeing-eye puppies, an interview with a vet about the job and training of a vet, book suggestions for good reading about pets, pets in sports, original poems about pets, common health problems of pets and how to avoid them, and a true story about a pet who was a hero. All feature stories had to use information from at least three sources, be accurate in information, show how pets and people are interdependent, help the audience understand and appreciate pets more fully, and use the class "careful writer rules." Students could use illustrations for their work but were not required to do so. The teacher, with assistance from the school's media specialist, helped students access resources for their writing, including websites, videos, magazines, books, and people the students could interview.

Because of the large number of articles produced by the students, there were three "issues" of the magazine, and students worked in one of three teams to produce them. All students either (1) took a copy of the magazine to a 1st, 2nd, or 3rd grade class, introduced it to them, and provided them with a feedback form to share their opinions about the magazine; or (2) went to one of the classrooms to retrieve the magazine and feedback from the students and to thank them for reading it and providing feedback. Students created the feedback form, worked on editing and revising their work, and practiced their oral presentations for the classes in their editorial teams.

Ultimately, each student prepared oral presentations for a "panel of magazine readers and pet fans." The presentations had to demonstrate that the student's magazine work had shown how pets and people are interdependent, how the pet is like and unlike a counterpart in the wild, and how the animal's structure affects how it functions. The presentations also had to explain how the student had used resources to get information for the magazine pieces, and to use complete sentences and details to support student explanations. The "magazine editor" gave students summative feedback and grades on their magazine pieces, and the "expert panel" gave students summative feedback and grades on their oral presentations. Because of the age of the students, the teacher gave "grades" with descriptors like "Very Good," "Good," and "Not Yet." It would be possible to use more traditional letter grades, a plus-check-minus system, one-two-three stars, or simply to indicate with a check which KUDs a student had demonstrated competently.

Also, because of the age of the students, there were not specific task assignment sheets. Instead, the teacher used "to-do" charts posted in the room to remind students of requirements, due dates, criteria for success, and other details about their work.

The assessment addresses the following KUDs:

Know:
- Key vocabulary: *environment, interdependence, ecosystem, domesticated animal, structure and function, survival needs, compare and contrast*
- Basic survival needs of animals: food, shelter, protection from danger
- Ways in which pets are like and different from animals in the wild
- Ways in which pets and people are interdependent

Understand:
- Pets must have their basic needs met in order to be healthy and have good lives.
- The way in which an animal is shaped affects many of the ways it functions.
- Pets are part of ecosystems that affect their lives and health.
- Pets are dependent upon people for health and survival.
- Pets and people can make one another's lives better.
- People have a responsibility to care for the pets they bring in to their lives.

Be able to do:
- Identify (classify) a pet with its animal family and explain why it is part of that animal family.
- Compare and contrast pets with animals from the same animal family in the wild.
- Write explanatory text to inform a specific audience.
- Write narrative text that recounts an event or explains thoughts or feelings in a logical order.
- Orally explain important ideas with supporting details to an audience.
- Use complete sentences in writing and speaking.

Related Standards
Students will . . .
- Comprehend informational text.
- Write informative/explanatory texts in which they introduce a topic, use facts and definitions to develop points, and provide a concluding statement or section.

- Write narratives in which they recount a well-elaborated event or short sequence of events; include details to describe actions, thoughts, and feelings; use temporal words to signal event order; and provide a sense of closure.

- Tell a story or recount an experience with appropriate facts and relevant, descriptive details, speaking audibly in coherent sentences.

- Produce complete sentences when appropriate to task and situation in order to provide requested detail or clarification.

- Strengthen writing as needed by revising and editing.

Notes from the Editor

To the Author _____

How You Did with Getting and Organizing Information	How You Did with Showing Big Ideas About Animals	How You Did with Careful Writer Rules
• Used at least three resources? • Gathered and used accurate information? • Explained your ideas in a logical way readers could follow and learn from? • Provided supporting details for your ideas? **Grade**	• Compared and contrasted your pet with similar animals in the wild? • Showed how pets and people are interdependent? • Showed how an animal's structure affects the way it functions? • Helped readers understand and appreciate pets more fully? **Grade**	• Used complete sentences? • Used capital letters to begin sentences and for proper nouns? • Used apostrophes for contractions and to show possession? • Used correct punctuation at the end of sentences? • Used correct spelling? • Revised your work to make it better? **Grade**
Keep working on	**Keep working on**	**Keep working on**

Expert Panel Feedback

Author and Presenter _____

How Well Did You . . .	Our Comments
Explain how you wrote about big ideas? • Pets and people are interdependent. • Your pet is like and different from similar animals in the wild. • The way an animal is shaped affects its function. *You did all of these well.* _____ *You did these but had some places that weren't clear enough.* _____ *You didn't do all of these well.* *Explain how you used resources to make your work accurate and interesting?* • Tell how you used resources to write your articles so they would be accurate and interesting. • Speak in complete sentences in your explanation. *You did both of these well.* _____ *You spoke in compete sentences but were not clear about how you used resources in your writing.* _____ *You explained some about how you used resources, but didn't always use complete sentences.* _____ *You did neither of these well.* _____ *Communicate with the panel?* • Present your ideas in a logical and easy-to-follow way. • Use details to support your explanations. • Speak clearly and loudly enough for us to hear and understand you. *You did all of these well.* _____ *You did these but had some places that weren't clear enough.* _____ *You didn't do all of these well.* _____	

Differentiation in Scenario 3

Differentiation based on student interests occurred in two ways. First, students could select a short contribution to the magazine based on particular interests. Second, when the teacher assigned students the feature-length articles, she created topics for each student based in part on that student's interests. Differentiation based on learning profile occurred as students might have elected to use images, charts, music, writing, or other options in their shorter contributions. Differentiation based on student readiness took place in several ways: (1) the teacher provided short-piece options requiring varied levels of thinking and writing complexity; (2) the teacher assigned feature-length pieces based in part on student readiness and topic complexity; (3) resources for research were in varied formats and at varied readability levels; (4) the teacher assigned editing groups and oral presentation practice groups that were sometimes more homogeneous and sometimes more heterogeneous so that students were able to get feedback from and examine the work of a variety of peers; and (5) students who had difficulty organizing and expressing ideas used a template for preparing their oral presentations to the expert panel, whereas students who were more comfortable with organization and oral presentation only consulted the "to-do" chart that included the elements required in the presentation. In all instances, the KUDs or content goals remained the same across options.

The teachers who generated these three summative assessments worked in quite different contexts and with different content. All three, however, adhered to some important principles about summative measures of student learning. The assessments are rich and call on students to understand and apply what they are learning rather than only to reproduce knowledge or skills. All three assessments clearly reflect KUDs that were known to students and teacher alike and that were evident during instruction (there is no "gotcha" testing). All students were called up to demonstrate proficiency with the same essential knowledge, understanding, and skill; but the format of the assessments also provided enough flexibility to allow for student differences with the intent of enabling each student to demonstrate as fully as possible what he or she had learned during the units of study. Further, the teacher assessed student responses against a common rubric or set of criteria rather than comparing students to one another. Application of these principles to summative assessment makes this part of the teaching-learning cycle more transparent, meaningful, and accessible for students than assessments that depart markedly from the principles. These examples suggest that quality summative assessment strongly resembles quality teaching.

6

Assessment, Grading, and Differentiation

Most kids never talk about it, but a lot of the time, bad grades make them feel dumb, and almost all the time it's not true. And good grades can make other kids think that they're better, and that's not true either. And then all the kids start competing and comparing. . . . And the people who are supposed to help kids, they don't. They just add more pressure and keep making up more and more tests.

—Andrew Clements, *The Report Card*

At the beginning of my (Carol's) third year of teaching, a very quiet, and evidently very courageous, small boy whispered something to me in the hall during the class change on the sixth day of school. His barely articulated words were lost in the chatter and energy of several hundred students moving from second period to third. After several failed attempts to have him speak louder and for me to listen "harder," I heard what he was saying. I thought he was asking me to help him open his locker—a predictable request for 7th graders who were new to lockers and middle school. What he was saying to me, however, reflected a need far more profound and challenging for both of us. What he whispered to the very tall lady he had never seen before was this: "I can't read." He was 15 and, as I learned from his crumpled class schedule, he was about to join my 7th grade language arts class composed of thirty-five 12-year-olds. He had missed the first week of school. He could not yet write the entire alphabet.

A herd of questions trampled through my brain. How did he get this far if he can't read? (*Irrelevant question. He's mine.*) How do you teach reading? (*Also irrelevant. No time for a course right now. Figure it out.*) Do I let the other kids know he has a special need or do I try to disguise it? (*How do I help a 15-year-old nonreader feel a sense of belonging and dignity in a 7th grade class that's based on reading?*) How do I find time to teach him? (*What happens if I quit paying attention to the other 34 kids in order to work with him?*) Where do I seat him in the room? (*Next to a good reader who can help him? Near my desk so I can get to him quickly?*) What materials do I use to help him learn to read? (*Nearly everything in our classroom is written at approximately grade level.*)

The questions that came to me from nowhere and in an instant are the baseline questions of what we now call differentiated instruction. For the next 18 years that I continued to teach in public school, I spent much of the time trying to find the best possible answers to those questions. Since then, I've spent my "second life" as a university teacher continuing to answer them with my colleagues and with teachers in classrooms across the world.

The boy's name was Golden. He provided me with a golden moment as a teacher. He made it impossible for me not to deal with the reality of student learning differences that were already quite evident to me before he arrived in my world. I understood the trust he had placed in me with his whispered confession. Now it was no longer possible for me to look past the range of needs in my classroom. Because of him, I had to figure out how to proactively deal with them. I didn't get a lot of sleep that year, but I became a much better teacher; and during all the years that followed, I was a much better steward of what my students brought to school with them.

By year's end, Golden was reading at a solid 3rd grade level. By any mandate that all students meet standard competencies by an arbitrary date in the spring, no matter their starting points, Golden would have been a failure—and so would I. But I still believe that my grandest accomplishment as a teacher was working with Golden in a coherent and sustained way so that together, we moved him forward as a reader more than three grade levels in one school year.

One question Golden's presence evoked in me was harder to answer than the rest. That question was "How do I grade him?"

I knew from the outset that the "traditional" and often revered system of grades and report cards created an undertow that threatened to swallow up any progress he made in school. Understanding that clearly, I felt that to be honest with him I needed to say the truth. "I want to help you see that you can read, Golden. I promise to work hard with you to make that happen. And I want you to promise to work hard with me. I do need to tell you, though, that no matter how hard you work, you won't be able to pass this class because to do that, you have to work at a level that is totally out of your reach this year. Still, I hope you'll come to school every day really excited to learn." I didn't say that to him explicitly, of course, but the ideas reflected in the "statement of truth" that ripped through my head in the hallway stayed with me.

What role should grades play with Golden and with the steady progression of struggling learners who came to me each year? And how about with students who are one or two or five years above grade level? Are there redemptive messages for them in our system of grades and report cards?

The purpose of this chapter is not to provide a digest of general grading theory and practice, but rather to investigate how best grading practices can guide teachers in understanding how we can (and how we shouldn't) think about grades and reporting so that students like Golden, students who are advanced, and students in between are well served by our grading practices.

A Bit of Background

Paul Dressel (1983) of Michigan State University defined grading in a way that likely represents the musings of many teachers at all levels around report card time at some point in their careers. A grade is "an inadequate report of an imprecise judgment of a biased and variable judge of the extent to which a student has attained an undefined level of mastery on an unknown proportion of an indefinite amount of material" (p. 12).

Grades have massive power in our schools and in the lives of the people whom we grade. We often speak of grading as though it were somehow sanctified—a thing that has to be as it has always been because to change the system would somehow create a disruption too great to bear. In truth, grades run through human filters. They are subjective. They are messy. It's probably healthier to give credence to Dressel's (1983) view than to the reverence that often prevails in conversations about grading.

Tonya is fond of saying that there is no real problem with grades and differentiation. The problem is that grading practices in general are such a mess that grades plus *anything* creates an issue. And yet, there is a literature on best practices in grading, developed by experts who study and research the topic carefully. Any consideration of grading and differentiation needs to begin with at least a brief explanation of the purposes of grading as defined by those with expertise in this area. The longer discussion that then follows on grading and differentiation ought also to reflect our best knowledge of sound grading practices that stem from the field of measurement, as opposed to emanating from "how we've always done things here." In regard to that last point, Ken O'Connor (2011) offers a relevant observation when he notes that although "we know more than we ever knew about how people learn, traditional grading practices persist. . . . These practices often not only result in ineffective communication, but may also may actually harm students and misrepresent their learning" (pp. xi–xii).

The purpose of grades, strictly speaking, is "to communicate information about a pupil's academic achievement. . . . Grading is a process in which a teacher transforms assessment data into meaningful information about pupil performance that is conveyed to pupils, parents, and others" (Airasian, 1997, p. 261). This brief explanation highlights three elements worth remembering. First, the primary goal of grading should be to help parents and students (as well as other stakeholders) know where a student currently stands in terms of academic achievement, with achievement defined as "performance measured against accepted published standards and learning outcomes" (O'Connor, 2011, p. 7)—in other words, to communicate clearly what a student knows, understands, and can do at a particular time. Second, to achieve that purpose, the information communicated and the method of communication must be clear to those who use it. Third, the grading process is a separate stage in assessment from administering and providing feedback on or scoring student work. In regard to the latter point, O'Connor (2011) distinguishes between "marks" and "grades." Marks, he suggests, are numbers or letters teachers put on student work that may later become part of a grade. A grade, on the other hand, is a symbol reported at a designated time as a summary statement of a student's performance.

Despite the assertion that grades exist to communicate to students, their parents, and others who need the information, grades are used for multiple purposes, including, but by no means limited to, communication of current student academic performance. These additional purposes include (1) ranking students (for example, computing class rank and identifying a class valedictorian); (2) motivating students to learn, or punishing them; (3) grouping, sorting, or placing students in classes; (4) providing teachers with information for instructional planning; and (4) teacher and program evaluation (Brookhart, 2004; O'Connor, 2011). These uses of grades have conflicting purposes and suggest different approaches to the grading process. Using grades for *all* of these purposes calls into question the validity of the grades for *any* of the purposes. More to the point, the swamp created by multipurpose grading makes it almost impossible for parents or students to be clear on what students know, understand, and can do at a given time relative to specified goals or to use that insight to support student learning.

It's critical, then, in making grades a positive and productive element in the teaching-learning-assessment cycle, that teachers and other educators understand fundamental principles of effective grading and work diligently to ensure that the principles are reflected in the grading and reporting process. The following section describes four important concepts that are foundational to good grading practices: error, reliability, validity, and teacher bias.

Foundations of Effective Grading

Understanding and addressing the concepts of error, reliability, validity, and teacher bias provides four legs of a stable grading process. The concepts should be present in teacher thinking any time the teacher is planning for, administering, reviewing, and reporting from assessments. The goal is to *increase* reliability and validity and to *reduce* error and teacher bias.

Jamie really loves reptiles and knows a great deal about them. Yesterday he took a test on reptiles in science class. He misunderstood the directions for one part of the test, however, and so his grade was only a 75. In truth, he knows much more than the test would have revealed even if he had not misunderstood the directions.

This brief scenario illustrates the concept of *error*. Because assessments are constructed by human beings and taken by human beings, they are always likely to be imperfect measures of a student's true knowledge of a topic. The difference between a score on an assessment and what a student really knows, understands, and can do related to that topic is called *error*. Error can occur for countless reasons: a poorly worded test item, a student's lack of fluency in the language in which assessment directions are written, a student's learning disability or attention problem, inadequate time for completing the assessment, a student who is hungry or not feeling well or is worried about home, a teacher who is intimidating to a student, and so on. A key goal of effective assessment is striving to eliminate error—and understanding that some error will remain nonetheless. Designing and administering assessments so that they get as close as possible to the student's "true score," or full understanding, should be a teacher's goal. Much of the rest of this chapter spotlights principles and practices for reducing error in assessments and grading.

Danielle received an *A* on the algebra test. She said to her friend as class ended, "Wow! This was my lucky day. I remembered exactly what the teacher did on the board and copied it from my brain to the paper. I guess that must have been the right thing to do, but if I had to take the test again today, I'd bomb!"

Danielle's experience calls into question the *reliability* of the test she took. Because she didn't understand what she had "learned," the chances are good that if she took the test again tomorrow or next week or in another teacher's class, her score would vary greatly. Reliability raises the question of consistency or stability of results. The more stable or consistent a student's score on multiple assessments on the same KUDs, the more reliable the measure, and the greater confidence teachers can have in the inferences they draw from the assessment. Using a greater variety of assessment formats and collaborating with colleagues to reach agreement about what really matters most in a particular topic or unit are two ways to increase reliability.

Mayan plans to talk with kids a year ahead of her in school when she takes her first big biology test next week. They'll know whether she should study the textbook or her notes. She's hoping it will be the textbook. She can sort of tell what that's about. When she takes notes in class, she often isn't sure if she's writing down the right things. Until she can figure out what a teacher wants, it's hard to know how to prepare for a test.

Mayan's plan to prepare for the biology test raises the issue of *validity*, or whether an assessment accurately measures what the teacher intends it to measure. If the teacher had been clear on the unit's KUDs, had taught with the KUDs at the forefront of his thinking, and had designed the test to measure those KUDs, it's much more likely that Mayan would have succeeded and that the test would have been valid. Using "backward design" (Wiggins & McTighe, 1998), making sure students are aware of KUDs and how they are reflected in instruction, targeting formative feedback on KUDs, and checking assessment items, directions, and criteria for success against specified KUDs are a few ways to increase validity of assessments.

Philip and Liza are looking at the grades and comments they just received on their summative projects on myths. They won't look at one another's work, but if an objective teacher compared them, it might raise the question of why Philip's grade is so much higher than Liza's. They both created myths that suggest an understanding of the purpose myths play in a culture, which is what the directions stressed. Philip's illustrations are terrific, however, and Liza's handwriting is not great. Besides, Philip has shown such an interest in the topic in class, and Liza has seemed bored much of the time. Philip's mom even brought in some resources on myths from other cultures and commented on how hard he was working on his project.

This scenario plays out in classrooms every day, not because teachers intend to be unfair, but because they are human. It's difficult *not* to favor the student who seems so invested in class—or whose parents do. It's hard *not* to bring some negativity to a grading task when a student consistently adds stress to a classroom. Teacher *bias* happens because teachers are people whose feelings, experiences, and expectations come to work with them every day. Wise teachers acknowledge the inevitability of bias and do everything they can to reduce it. Teachers can reduce bias as they establish clear criteria and rubrics or quality indicators for student work and systematically provide feedback or grades based directly on those goals and indicators. They can also reduce bias as they work with colleagues to be mindful of bias in the classroom and how it affects both teaching and learning.

In much of the remainder of the chapter, we provide principles and practices for quality assessment and grading. Look for references to *error, reliability, validity,* and *bias* in explanations. Think about the concepts also in regard to your own work. Working consistently to increase reliability and validity in assessments and to reduce error and teacher bias reflects a desire to engage in best-practice assessment. It also is highly likely to minimize most of the "problems" educators may assume exist with assessment and grading in an effectively differentiated classroom.

Issues Related to Assessment, Grading, and Differentiation

Probably the most frequently asked question about differentiation by educators around the world is "How would I grade it?" There is a broad, pervasive sense that differentiation and grading practices are somehow at odds with one another. In that vein, it's useful to think about issues related to assessment, grading, and differentiation in two categories: issues that are really misconceptions and issues that are fundamental to the philosophy and goals of differentiation.

Misconceptions

Two common issues with assessment, grading, and differentiation fall into the misconception category. The first has to do with content goals or KUDs, the second with a "standard" for grading and reporting.

Some educators think of differentiation as having different goals for different students. Not only does this perspective make teaching and learning much more confusing and complicated, but it turns grading into a nightmare. It's essential to know that defensible differentiation seeks to provide multiple pathways and support systems to the same content goals so that virtually all learners can achieve higher levels of success with the *same* essential knowledge, understanding, and skill. Thus a teacher in a differentiated classroom is not grading students on different goals (with the exception of students with certain IEPs), but rather will provide feedback and grades based on a student's status relative to the same KUDs.

Further, some educators feel as though differentiation calls on teachers to grade struggling students "easier" and advanced students "harder." That, too, is a misconception. Differentiation is not about jiggling grades. As we discuss with a bit more detail later in the chapter, virtually all students in a differentiated classroom should be graded against the same clearly delineated criteria (KUDs). What a differentiated classroom does is provide an environment that maximizes student opportunity to achieve and, when possible, move beyond those criteria.

Core Issues

Although some issues related to assessment, grading, and differentiation are, or ought to be, nonissues, at least three interrelated issues integral to the philosophy of differentiation are directly affected by assessment and grading practices. First, differentiation proposes that classroom practices—including assessment and grading—should be designed to contribute to a growth mind-set in students and teachers. Second, differentiation exists to keep students' success-to-effort ratios in balance—that is, students at all levels of proficiency clearly see that their hard work (effort) generally leads to visible success. Third, differentiation proposes that a sense of team, community, or collaboration is integral to student success—that students and teachers work together respectfully to support maximum growth for all. Many current grading practices—related to pre-assessment (or lack of it), to ongoing assessment, to summative assessment, to report cards—work directly against these three goals.

Commenting on the unspoken effect of grades, Earl (2003) reflects, "For some students, the certainty of praise and success in school has become a drug; they continually need more. For many other students, year upon year of 'not good enough' has eroded their intellectual self-confidence and resulted in a kind of mind-numbing malaise" (p. 15). Current assessment and grading practices are also counterproductive for a third group of students—those in the midranges of achievement who get the continual message that they are "just average" and not likely to change.

Needless to say, these three groups constitute a large proportion of the school population. Ways we teach, assess, and grade too frequently work against development of a belief that we can learn virtually anything necessary for success in school if we work at it and have a good support system. The way we teach, assess, and grade too frequently suggests to some students that effort rarely pays off, whereas to others it suggests that hard work is not necessary for achievement. Both messages are lethal to motivation. How we teach, assess, and grade too frequently creates winners and losers in the classroom and undercuts the sense that we are all stronger when we learn from and teach one another. Therefore, an effectively differentiated classroom is invested in assessment and grading practices that are in sync with responsive teaching practices— ones that clearly contribute to enlisting the effort of a full range of students to do the hard work of learning.

We also believe, however, that classrooms successful in maximizing the capacity of a broad range of students are built on best practices in *all* elements of teaching—learning environment, curriculum, instruction, classroom leadership and management, *and* assessment and grading. So the essential question for this chapter is this: Are there practices that reflect and support best-practice assessment and grading as well as the underpinnings of differentiation?

Our conclusion is that best practices in assessment and grading are fully compatible with and supportive of the goals of quality differentiation. That is, when educators implement the advice of experts in the field of measurement, there is no conflict with the philosophy and practice of differentiation related to assessment and grading. In fact, best-practice assessment and grading facilitates and enhances a robustly differentiated classroom.

Grading and reporting should be seen as particular moments that happen periodically in a much longer cycle of planning, teaching, learning, feedback, and measurement. Teaching and learning should be the primary focus of the classroom. Pre- and ongoing assessments inform the teaching-learning process. At key points in a unit of study, summative assessments measure student growth toward and beyond KUDs and result in marks entered into a gradebook. At the end of a designated marking period, the teacher converts marks into grades and communicates them on a report card. Grading and reporting should reflect and support good classroom practices, not dictate them.

Guiding Principles for Effective Grading Practices

Measurement and assessment experts generally agree on a number of attributes of effective grading practices. For example, grades should be consistent across classrooms (Brookhart, 2013). A focus on the same KUDs that serve as the basis for grades should be consistent across classrooms. That is, what matters most in teaching and assessment in one 4th grade math unit should be what matters most in teaching and assessment of the same unit in the other 4th grade classrooms. Grades should also be accurate. In other words, there should be no "mathematical distortions" resulting in an inaccurate picture of student status. Grades should be meaningful to those who receive them. In other words, grades should communicate clear and useful information. Finally, grades should support learning. That is, they should do the best possible job of communicating precisely what a student knows, understands, and can do at a particular time (O'Connor, 2011). Grades that are consistent, accurate, meaningful, and supportive of learning will necessarily reflect a teacher's successful efforts in increasing reliability and validity in the assessment and grading process, and minimizing error and teacher bias.

The principles that follow contribute to grades that are consistent, accurate, meaningful, and supportive of learning (Black & Wiliam, 1998; Earl, 2003; Hattie, 2012a; O'Connor, 2011; Tomlinson & McTighe, 2006; Wiggins, 1998). The principles necessarily involve formative and summative practices as well as the "grading moment" because those are all part of the assessment cycle. After a brief discussion of each principle is a statement about how the principle contributes to the foundational concepts of effective grading practice (reliability, validity, error, and bias) and to the descriptors of effective grading practice (consistent, accurate, meaningful, supportive of learning). There is also a statement about the role of the principle in addressing the differentiation-specific goals of developing a growth mind-set, balancing the student's success-to-effort ratio, and building classroom community.

1. Base Grades on Clearly Specified Learning Goals

It's a simple idea—the notion that students can hit any learning target that they can see and that holds still for them (Stiggins, 2001). Obvious though the idea may be, however, it's one we struggle to enact in classrooms. Virtually all teachers can specify what students will cover in a week or a unit of study and what students will do in a given sequence of learning. Few of us can specify with confidence and clarity what students should know, understand, and be able to do during those same time spans. Lacking that clarity before a unit ever begins, curriculum becomes a collection of amorphous information, lessons go off course, and assessments turn into a guessing game. On the other hand, when a teacher is clear about KUDs and how they work together to help learners make meaning of and use content, it's not a great leap to make sure students are clear about them as well. At that point, lessons have purpose and students understand that purpose; assessments are transparent vehicles for helping students see their proximity to the targets they know about and for helping them continue growth toward and beyond those targets; and grades communicate student status relative to known targets. Without clear KUDs and effective use of them in all aspects of instructional planning, learning targets wiggle or disappear from view. "Students become accustomed to receiving classroom teaching as an arbitrary sequence of exercises with no overarching rationale" (Black & Wiliam, 1998, p. 143). Grades become mysterious symbols accorded considerable power but of dubious worth.

Contribution to effective grading practices in general: This principle of clearly specifying KUDs increases reliability by providing consistency across classrooms, and it increases validity by ensuring that assessments measure what they are intended to measure. It decreases error by focusing students and the teacher on what matters most, and it decreases bias by providing specific criteria against which marking will occur.

Contribution to goals of differentiation: This principle increases the likelihood that student effort in learning and participation in assessments will result in success because there are clear targets and criteria for success. It also supports a growth mind-set because clear learning targets enable students to work with efficacy and confidence toward those goals. And it contributes to community by making clear the shared goals and achievement criteria toward which students can help one another progress.

2. Use Grades That Are Criterion Based, Not Comparative or Norm Based

When students are compared with one another, they come to believe the goal is competition rather than personal improvement. Often the result is that struggling students come to believe they lack the capacity for success, and high-achieving students conclude that success is an entitlement and not the result of commitment and hard work (Black & Wiliam, 1998). A teacher's aim should be to do everything possible to make sure all students achieve specified goals or criteria for success, not to sort and rank them. Teachers are increasingly effective with their professional work as more and more students succeed with specified criteria. Few of us would opt to sign on with a surgeon who believed in curing on a curve. Grading on a curve "is an artifact that bears no clear relation to valid standards, and indeed is psychometrically indefensible at the classroom level" (Wiggins, 1998, p. 248). It might provide some "information about a student's rank in a class, but does not speak to the student's academic achievement" (Marzano, 2010, p. 17).

Contribution to effective grading practices in general: This principle increases reliability by providing stable achievement criteria, and it increases validity by ensuring that grades are based on content goals rather than personal variables. It reduces bias that occurs as teachers attempt to compare individuals, and it reduces error that occurs as teachers attempt to compare individuals rather than assessing work according to stable criteria.

Contribution to goals of differentiation: This principle enables students to "compete against themselves" as they strive to achieve stable goals rather than feeling they will always suffer by being compared to more advanced students or that they must always be "at the top of the pack." By focusing on growth, it encourages a growth mind-set in all students. It balances the success-to-effort ratio by emphasizing personal growth rather than competition, and it contributes to community by reducing competition and diminishing a culture of winners and losers.

3. Don't Overgrade Student Work

Learning challenging content—really learning it so that it makes sense, is useful, and is transferable—takes hard work and lots of practice. Along the way to this kind of deep learning, false starts, mistakes, and redirection will necessarily occur. Grading everything students do discourages the very kind of grappling that is fundamental to complex thought and genuine understanding. It's important, then, to help students see a direct connection between what we ask them to do for practice at school and at home and their academic growth—between the quality of their practice and their developing competence. Young people routinely engage in strenuous practice to get better at basketball, soccer, playing a musical instrument, drawing, and so on. They literally "see" that the practice moves them forward. They don't expect or want a grade for every segment of practice because it is clear to them that the practice makes them more skilled when a "grading moment" (game, swim meet, recital, contest, exhibition) occurs. The endemic teacher comment that "Students won't do the work unless we grade it" points to a disconnect between practice and outcome in students' minds. Rather than solving the problem, grading everything students do perpetuates the problem. Grades should derive from summative, not formative, assessments. When we grade students while they are learning, they often see the grade as the end of learning (Hattie, 2012a).

Contribution to effective grading practices in general: This principle increases reliability and validity because it requires taking into consideration when student learning is likely to be more secure. It reduces error by providing time for practice to solidify learning rather than judging learning prematurely.

Contribution to goals of differentiation: This principle encourages a growth mind-set by focusing students on learning rather than premature judgment. It encourages struggling learners to persist by deferring judgment and advanced learners to accept meaningful challenge without fear of "losing points" before they've had a chance to develop competence, thus keeping the success-to-effort ratio balanced.

4. Use Only Quality Assessments

Quality assessments are associated with higher student achievement (Black & Wiliam, 1998), perhaps because those assessments suggest teachers whose planning and instruction are of high quality as well, and perhaps because such assessments encourage students to participate more enthusiastically in the learning process. Assessments are effective when they measure student proficiency on clearly designated learning goals (KUDs) that are known to students, and when they are carefully aligned with teaching and learning. No trick questions or "gotcha" items! It's important also that the method of assessing students be a match for the kind of learning we mean to assess. For example, a thoughtfully constructed multiple-choice or fill-in-the-blank test is often well suited to assessing student *knowledge*. A performance assessment or well-designed product assessment is typically better for determining students' understanding of content and their ability to apply and transfer that *understanding*. It's important, too, to ensure that the assessment provides ample opportunity for students to reveal their proficiency with a particular segment of content. In other words, offering only one item on an important idea may increase the chance that a student appears to misunderstand the idea when, in fact, the student simply misunderstood that one question. It's also critical to con-sider assessment-related issues that can increase error in the assessment. For instance, a student may not be able to read the directions well enough to follow them, or may have difficulty following multistep directions and the assessment contains five steps, or may consistently need additional time to complete an assessment, or may lack home resources required for a product assessment. Parental assistance also increases error in grades. In such instances, the assessment falls short of the critical goal of revealing what a student knows, understands, and can do related to essential content.

Contribution to effective grading practices in general: This principle increases reliability across classrooms, and it increases validity by focusing the assessment on what matters most. It reduces error by adequately sampling important knowledge, understanding, or skill; eliminating "gotcha" items; and addressing student variables that can result in inaccurate representations of mastery.

Contribution to goals of differentiation: This principle contributes to a balanced suc-cess-to-effort ratio and growth mind-set by ensuring a focus on essential and specified goals known to the student; adequate sampling of student knowledge, understanding, and skill; and accounting for student variables that can skew performance.

5. Reduce "Grade Fog"

Grade fog arises from anything teachers do in the teaching-learning-assessment grading cycle that muddles the meaning or clarity of the grade. Recall that a grade should communicate as clearly as possible to students, parents, and other stakeholders what a student knows, understands, and can do at a given point in time. Well before time for grading in a teaching-learning-assessment cycle, grade fog begins to appear when teachers deduct points from an assessment because a piece of work isn't neat, because it is late, or because the student's name is left off the paper. Grade fog continues to obscure the meaning of the grade when teachers add extra credit to a grade, include bonus points, count attendance as part of a grade, include group scores, incorporate student behavior in a grade, or count homework in grades. All of those relatively common practices make considerably less clear what that student's level of academic mastery actually is through the grade that is eventually communicated. It's not uncommon for a student to receive an *A* on a summative exam at the end of a marking period but a *C* on his report card because he turned in homework only sporadically. It's not unheard of for an eager child with weak reading skills to turn in extra-credit work and receive a *B* on a report card in language arts when the student's actual skill level would indicate a *C* or a *C-* would be more accurate. When a grade serves multiple masters, it serves none of them well. If you're thinking, "Yes, but homework teaches responsibility" or "It's important for students to work effectively in a group," we agree. The discussion of 3-P grading (Principle 8) will address those issues.

Contribution to effective grading practices in general: This principle increases reliability and validity and decreases error by focusing assessment results and grades on important and articulated goals rather than less salient variables. It reduces teacher bias by maintaining a grading focus on important and articulated *content* goals rather than on *student* variables that are less salient.

Contribution to goals of differentiation: This principle helps develop a student-growth mind-set by keeping the focus on learning and learning outcomes rather than on variables extraneous to learning, and by minimizing grades as rewards or punishments.

6. Eliminate "Mathematical Grade Fog"

Two mathematical processes commonly used in grading are responsible for both imprecise communication about student learning and unnecessary student discouragement. One of those is giving zeros when work is missing or if students have cheated on assessments. "Grades are broken when zeros are entered into a student's academic record for missing evidence or as punishment for transgressions. . . . Use alternatives, such as reassessing to determine real achievement, or use 'I' for Incomplete or Insufficient

Evidence" (O'Connor, 2011, p. 95). Guide students in developing plans for making up missed work. Develop compensatory alternatives to zeros for significant infractions such as cheating.

Zeros are problematic on at least three levels. First, they have such an extreme effect on grades that it's difficult for a student's grade to ever really recover. Second, rather than teaching students accountability for their work, zeros actually teach students they don't really have to do work if they are willing to accept a zero instead. Sadly, many discouraged students accept the zero and never master the goals attached to missing work. Finally, zeros significantly discourage student investment in the learning process—a particularly costly outcome for students who already find school to be distasteful and the prospects of academic success to be implausible.

A second source of mathematical grade fog is the process of averaging grades. Grades that reflect a student's "mean" score, asserts O'Connor (2011), are "mean" to students because they overemphasize outlier scores (most commonly, low ones) and distort the report of a student's actual learning. It may be that some assessments contain easier—or more complex—items than others and therefore should not receive the same weight in grading. Likewise, some assessments may measure more important concepts than others. In other instances, a performance assessment might provide a more accurate representation of a student's understanding of content than a multiple-choice test given at about the same time. There are many reasons why not all assessments in a marking period are equal in importance and therefore why they should not be weighted equally in computing grades.

Rather than computing a mean, it may make better sense to use a student's median (middle) score or to use the student's mode (most often earned) score. In fact, a number of experts in grading (e.g., Guskey, 1996; O'Connor, 2011; Wiggins, 1998) suggest that it is unwise to use *any* mechanical formula or process for computing grades. They advise that teachers understand that grading is judgment based and that effective grading practices call on teachers to use their own best professional judgment in determining what grade most appropriately represents a student's achievement at a given time. A letter grade on a report card appears definitive and objective, but it actually covers up an array of judgments, ambiguities, and questions that need to be aired and debated (Wiggins, 1998).

Contribution to effective grading practices in general: This principle increases reliability and validity of grades by maintaining a focus on what students actually know, understand, and can do at key points in the learning cycle. It reduces error by providing a more accurate picture of student proficiency related to specified goals, and it reduces bias by decoupling behavior and grades.

Contribution to goals of differentiation: This principle supports development of a growth mind-set and a balanced success-to-effort ratio by maintaining a focus on learning. It avoids additional discouragement of struggling, alienated, or disenfranchised students by removing behavior from grades.

7. Grade More Heavily Later in a Grading Cycle Rather Than Earlier

This principle addresses the need for practice in learning as does Principle 3, but from a slightly different vantage point. The purpose of this principle is illustrated well by Derrick, a student from a low-income home who struggled to do well in school during much of his adolescence. To his credit, he continued the struggle and ultimately went to college and was quite successful there. He reflected as a college student on things that made it very hard for him to persist in school when many of his friends did not. The hardest times for him, he recalled, were numerous instances when teachers said to him that his report card grade was lower than they'd hoped. Their comments often went something like this: "You made an *A* on the exam, but you had a couple of test grades early in the quarter that pulled your grade down." Derrick said, "I always felt like I was being punished for keeping on somehow." It would have been great if teachers had said, "I know you're working hard and it's paying off. At the beginning of the quarter, your marks were lower, but you kept working and mastered the content by exam time. That shows me you've learned what you needed to learn. Good for you!" When a student gets better marks later in a marking period, it suggests effort and growth—two prime predictors of success. Earlier deficiencies *in the same content* ought not to erode the student's growth or discourage persistence. The fact that a student learned more as the quarter proceeded should also indicate that the teacher taught in such a way that she was able to help the student overcome initial difficulties.

Contribution to effective grading practices in general: This principle increases validity of grades by emphasizing student performance after adequate opportunity to learn rather than before learning is complete. It decreases error by avoiding premature assessments of student "learning."

Contribution to goals of differentiation: This principle increases students' growth mind-set and success-to-effort ratio by recognizing student persistence in learning. It increases teachers' growth mind-set by calling attention to student growth rather than focusing on earlier deficiencies.

8. When It's Time for Report Cards, Use 3-P Grading

Earlier in this chapter we asserted that teachers and other educators use grades to represent so many and often conflicting elements that the grades become essentially useless in communicating clearly what students know, understand, and can do. That reality, affirmed by many experts in grading, does not, however, negate the fact that teachers want to help students develop in multiple ways—including, but not limited to, taking responsibility, collaborating with peers, striving for quality work, and so on. Some of these factors are important in developing a growth mind-set and in becoming a successful learner. Experts in measurement agree that information about a variety of aspects of student development can be useful to parents and students. What they disagree with is lumping a mishmash of information into a single symbol. "When we try to pack a wide variety of student characteristics into one grade, that grade is not a valid reflection of any one of them" (Stiggins, 2001, p. 441). This practice, Stiggins (2006) asserts, results in hodgepodge grades that produce a confusing amalgam that is impossible to interpret and likely presents an inaccurate picture of a student's proficiency.

One solution to the dilemma is to practice what is called "3-P grading"—that is, to report separate grades for a student's performance or product (our best information about what the student knows, understands, and can do), the student's process (habits of mind and work that characterize successful people in a wide range of endeavors and that we hope to help students develop), and the student's progress (student growth in specified KUDs since the prior marking period) (Guskey, 2006; Stiggins, 2006; Wiggins, 1998). *It should go without saying that the three Ps should not be averaged into one report card grade.* Rather, they should be reported separately and with clear indicators of what each element represents. The product or performance grade unambiguously reports only student status on KUDs. The process grade includes things like whether the student persists in the face of difficulty, uses feedback to improve performance, asks for clarification when needed, seeks multiple perspectives on issues, and so on. If a teacher is convinced that homework for a student is appropriately challenging and useful in promoting that student's academic development, and that it is the work of the student alone and not the parent, it can be included in a process grade and as an indicator of accepting responsibility for assigned work.

The 3-P approach to grading is tightly aligned with the growth-mind-set message that if individuals work hard and intelligently to master specified goals (process), they will continue to grow toward those goals (progress), until they master those goals (product or performance) and perhaps even move beyond them. Effective 3-P grading requires teachers to develop and share thoughtful continuums of progress in their content areas, which might begin with learning progressions such as those discussed in Chapter 4. In addition, it's important to develop and share indicators or rubrics that describe characteristics of productive habits of mind and work (process). A useful source for understanding the relationship between habits of mind and success and for building descriptors of habits of mind in the classroom is the work of Art Costa and Bena Kallick on this topic—for example, *Learning and Leading with Habits of Mind: 16 Essential Characteristics for Success* (2008). Likewise, of course, as we have stressed throughout the book, it is essential that teachers provide clear descriptors of performance targets so that students and parents understand the game plan for schoolwork and homework—and the meaning of a performance or product grade. In addition to increasing student understanding of and efficacy with the learning process and parent clarity about the meaning of grades, working from reasoned and clearly articulated descriptors of process, progress, and performance—especially when those descriptors are shared across classrooms—helps teachers increase reliability and validity of grades while decreasing error and bias.

It's useful in the context of 3-P grading to distinguish between effort and process. Teachers with a growth mind-set encourage students to work hard, or to contribute effort, in order to grow academically. That encouragement is well founded in terms of the critical role of effort in success. When it comes to grading, however, the vocabulary needs to shift a bit. It's not possible to observe effort accurately, and we can't (or ought not try to) grade what we can't observe. So in the context of 3-P grading, there is a vocabulary shift from *effort* to *process*. We can observe that a student willingly revises his work to improve its quality. We can observe that a student seeks help when she is stuck on some aspect of her work. We can observe that a student develops a time line for completing a complex task and adheres to it. Those sorts of "habits of mind and work" are indicators of the sorts of "intelligent processes" that are associated with successful people. Good grading practice requires that we use visible indicators. However, it's also extremely important that teachers not just generally talk with students about "hard work" or "effort," but rather that they teach students the attributes of work that make effort pay off in terms of performance and guide students in developing and enacting those attributes.

Educators can certainly design report cards around 3-P grading. Lacking such report cards (or as districts move in that direction), teachers can and should talk with parents and students about 3-P grading, making clear the value of understanding a student's position in each area at a given time and using the knowledge to support student growth. Teachers can report a student's performance, process, and progress in a report card comment section, on an addendum to a report card, in regularly scheduled e-mail communication, during parent night conferences, as a part of student portfolios, through student-developed self-reports, and in other ways.

Contribution to effective grading practices in general: This principle increases validity of grades and decreases error by separating performance from process and progress.

Contribution to goals of differentiation: This principle reinforces the message for the full spectrum of students that working hard and intelligently leads to growth and ultimately to mastery and even moving beyond important goals.

9. Open Up the Assessment and Grading Process

Involve students in the grading and reporting process as well as in pre- and formative assessment. Students at a young age should be able to connect the dots between their learning goals, their work in class and at home, summative work, grades, and reporting. They should be able to explain to themselves, their teacher, and their parents when their habits of work and mind contribute to their growth, when they don't, and what they can do to focus their efforts to benefit their growth. Further, don't make report cards the only communication with parents and students about student learning. Ongoing and shared conversation about students' personal and academic development provides opportunity for everyone involved to be an informed contributor to student success. Grading can be demystified and, more important, shared ownership of the learning process is possible as teachers emphasize useful feedback for learning and deemphasize the primacy of a single grade issued four times a year.

Contribution to effective grading practices in general: The principle of open dialogue should contribute to increased validity of grades as teachers, students, and parents develop a common understanding of goals and processes.

Contribution to goals of differentiation: This principle encourages a growth mind-set by helping students gain understanding of, responsibility for, and partnership in assessment and reporting throughout the learning cycle.

A Final Caveat About Grades and Differentiation

It's easy to succumb to the notion that somehow grades and grading practices can solve significant classroom problems. For example, teachers seem to hold out hope that grades will motivate reluctant learners to invest more energy in learning, or that they will continue to elicit the eager participation of high-achieving students, or that they will encourage "absent-minded" students to pay attention more regularly. In reality, grades often reinforce a sense of hopelessness in struggling learners, motivate students with good grades to get more good grades rather than to learn, and appear irrelevant to students who have their own agendas.

Students bring to the classroom a variety of differences in academic orientation, in-school and out-of-school experiences, interests, ways in which they prefer to learn, fundamental language skills, and so on. Regardless of these individual differences, all students are expected to master the same content standards unless there are formal plans on record that indicate otherwise. The dual reality of student differences juxtaposed with common expectations requires educators to create classrooms that respect those differences and are thus structured to provide varied ways in which students can meet common content expectations.

It is effective attention to student variance that encourages students to reach for successively higher levels of proficiency, provides an environment that supports the risk of learning, and presents students with a reason for optimism that each day will result in incremental success toward important goals. Neither evidence nor common sense suggests that grades are effective mechanisms for "fixing" student differences. The best-case scenario for grades is that they present students and parents with accurate and intelligible representations of development in a context where all efforts are aimed at moving students as far forward as possible from where they begin in a content area by addressing their varied readiness needs, interests, and approaches to learning.

In the field of measurement, instruction is referred to as a "treatment" students receive. Designing that treatment to maximize the capacity of each learner is the core mission of differentiated instruction and ought to be the core mission of the educational endeavor. Quality grading practices facilitate that mission but cannot replace it.

Effective Grading in a Differentiated Classroom: A Quick Review

Grading is a process that occurs at designated end points in a much longer cycle of teaching, learning, and assessment. The goal of grades is to communicate clearly to students, parents, and other stakeholders a student's status relative to clearly delineated learning goals. Because grading is done by humans, it involves judgment, subjectivity, and error. It's important to acknowledge that reality, which has both benefits and liabilities for students. Teachers who seek to use best-practice assessment and grading strive to ensure reliability and validity in their assessments and grades while also working to reduce error and bias.

Certain principles support quality grading and associated assessment practices and generally increase reliability and validity while also reducing error and bias. They not only reflect recommended practices in grading and assessment but also support three goals of a differentiated classroom: developing growth mind-sets in students and teachers, maintaining a balance in student success-to-effort ratios, and building classroom community. The principles are as follows:

1. Base grades on clearly specified learning goals.

2. Use grades that are criterion based, not comparative or norm based.

3. Don't overgrade student work.

4. Use only quality assessments.

5. Reduce "grade fog."

6. Eliminate "mathematical grade fog."

7. Grade more heavily later in a grading cycle rather than earlier.

8. When it's time for report cards, use 3-P grading.

9. Open up the assessment and grading process.

Cases in Point

Following are four classroom scenarios related to grading. The first three provide some structured-response options and one open-ended response option to guide your thinking about the grading situation described in the scenario. Whichever option you select as your preferred response, articulate your reasons for the response in relation to the guidelines presented in this chapter. The fourth scenario is messier because it contains more variables and is completely open-ended. There, too, think about what you understand to be effective grading practices. Use that understanding to develop advice you'd give to the teacher in the scenario.

Scenario 1: 10th Grade History

In a 10th grade U.S. History I class, Mrs. Wright's second 9-week report card grade is based on four quizzes, two in-class tests, and an-out-of-class project that counts as 30 percent of the grade. Carter obtained an A- average on the quizzes and the two tests but has not turned in the project, which is three days late, despite repeated requests from Mrs. Wright. In this situation, Mrs. Wright should (a) assign Carter a zero for the project and average his quiz grades, the test grades, and the project grade, which would give him a D average for his report card; (b) assign Carter a lower grade than an A-, taking off some points for his lack of effort in getting the project turned in on time; (c) exclude the missing project grade from calculating overall grades for the nine weeks; or (d) do something else.

Scenario 2: 7th Grade Science

Mr. Hernandez teaches in a heterogeneously grouped 7th grade science classroom. Zoe is an advanced learner who thinks clearly, asks thoughtful questions, and writes well. In looking at Zoe's recent work, Mr. Hernandez notices that she is not doing her best work, even though her work is better than that of the rest of her classmates. Zoe's effort has been minimal, but because of her academic ability, her work is reasonably good. In this situation, Mr. Hernandez should (a) lower Zoe's grade because she did not put effort into class work (b) give Zoe a lower grade in hopes that it encourages her to work harder (c) grade Zoe on the quality of the work; or (d) do something else.

Scenario 3: Pre-algebra

Ms. Barrett teaches a pre-algebra class that is heterogeneously grouped. Two exams contribute to the nine-week grade. In calculating Jose's grade, Ms. Barrett notices that Jose achieved a C on the first exam and an A on the second exam. In this situation, Ms. Barrett should (a) assign Jose an overall grade of B, which is the average of his two test scores; (b) assign Jose an overall grade of *A*, since he showed improvement on the second exam; or (c) do something else.

Scenario 4: 3rd Grade Reading

Ms. Atkinson teaches 3rd grade and has several students in her class who are lagging behind in development of reading skills. Tia is an English language learner who is very shy and has great difficulty participating in class. Sammy and Chase seem immature for their age group. They have difficulty paying attention in class, often disturb other students trying to work, and rarely complete assignments without considerable prodding. When she prods, however, their work is marginally acceptable. Daniel has a weak vocabulary, which is a particular problem in reading nonfiction materials, although he decodes reasonably well and works hard in class. Millie is a puzzle. Sometimes she seems to read fluently. However, she frequently refuses to read aloud in small groups or individually with the teacher. Her written work does not indicate good comprehension, yet she can sometimes answer comprehension questions in class that no one else can answer.

As the grading period is ending, Ms. Atkinson realizes the students have roughly the same marks on the work in her gradebook, yet when she thinks about the students, she feels that Tia is working at a lower level of reading proficiency than the others. She also wants to encourage Daniel's hard work and wants his grade to be part of that encouragement. She doesn't know how to report on Millie's uneven profile. She knows Sammy and Chase can do better work than they generally do. How would you advise Ms. Atkinson as she begins to determine grades and make out her report cards for these students in the current marking period?

If we are good stewards of the opportunity to teach young people, we continue throughout our careers to develop and work from a grounded philosophy that dignifies the students we teach with thoughtful, challenging, and supportive pedagogy. We need to take care that we see grading as a reflection and extension of rather than a departure from the principles of informed, defensible, and nurturing classroom practice.

7

A Look Back and Ahead

The three great essentials to achieve anything worthwhile are, first, hard work; second, stick-to-itiveness; third, common sense.

—Thomas Edison

Imagine saving the money for a house you've hoped to build some day, going to an architect with ideas for house plans swirling in your brain, and having the architect say, "Well, that's nice, but I only build one floor plan and it's not the one you have in mind." Imagine feeling awful and going to a physician who says, "I understand what you're saying about how you feel, but today I'm prepared to treat only one set of symptoms, and it's not the set you brought with you into the office." Imagine a tax specialist who knows how to complete only one tax form, or a restaurant that carries only one item, served in one way, or a landscaper who plants only azaleas. And imagine someone's child—perhaps your child—going into a classroom where the teacher says—in actions, if not words—"I'm prepared to teach only one kind of kid, and it isn't you."

Differentiation, effectively implemented, extends our reach as teachers. It professionalizes us. It enables us to convey this message to all students who enter our classroom: "There's room for you to learn here as you are!"

Recently one of our University of Virginia teacher education students who had just completed his teaching internship took a class on differentiated instruction and summarized his understanding of the concept relatively early in the course. He began by saying he thought differentiation was a series of common-sense decisions made by teachers with a student-first orientation. He continued by delineating those decisions as he saw them. First, teachers have to be continually focused on creating a classroom environment that invites all kinds of students—every student—to take the risk of learning. If we fall short there, he suggested, everything else we do is diminished. Then, he reasoned, teachers have to continue to craft and hone the curriculum they teach so that it engages

141

young minds and prepares them to understand and take wise action in the world around them. If we fall short there, we've wasted human capacity. Next, he proposed that teachers who are invested in their students and care deeply about the content they teach will want to know how learning is progressing for each student in their care. Therefore, they regularly use formative assessment to be informed about how things are going for each learner. If we fall short there, we are teaching with our eyes closed. Next, he concluded, teachers would do something about what the formative assessments revealed to them. In other words, they'd attend to students' readiness needs, their interests, and their learning preferences in order to increase the prospects that each student could grow academically as much as possible. To fall short there is to deny students access to success. Finally, he concluded, teachers have to learn to guide a classroom in which more than one thing at a time can happen smoothly and efficiently when necessary. To fall short there is to render useless the other four elements.

The young man who offered this "common sense" definition of differentiation had written out his explanation because he felt he must be missing some critical element in the concept as his understanding was developing. When he received feedback indicating he understood the framework of differentiation well and expressed it clearly, he looked puzzled—almost displeased. "Well," he said, "if that's all differentiation is, why doesn't everyone do it?"

The ideas he understood to be at the heart of differentiation made so much sense to him that he simply couldn't figure out why he didn't see it all around him during his student-teaching experiences. Ultimately, he concluded his musing with one final question. "I mean, which of these elements would teachers think are unimportant?"

The correct answer to his rhetorical question is likely that most teachers would think all of those elements make sense—even common sense. But common sense is hidden from view by old habits and ways of responding to the world. Isaac Asimov, in his 1950 novel *I, Robot*, reflects that the obvious things can be the most difficult to see. People admonish us that the thing we're missing is as obvious as the nose on our face. How much of your nose can you see, he ponders, unless someone puts a mirror in front of you!

We hope this book helps you see a bit more clearly the common-sense role of assessment in a differentiated classroom. We hope it has held a mirror up to your practice so it's a bit easier to see where your work aligns with best-practice assessment—and where it does not. We hope, too, that the book has helped you develop your understanding of how the five key elements in a differentiated classroom interact to provide optimum conditions for learning for a broad variety of learners.

This book has focused on one of the five fundamental elements of differentiation: use of assessment to inform instructional planning. Figure 7.1 summarizes some key points from the book about that element. Blatant common sense characterizes the work of teachers who assume they need to monitor the learning of their students and then adjust their teaching in ways that respond meaningfully to students' varied learning journeys. Recall that assessment is only formative when teachers use the assessment results to teach more effectively than they would have if they had not had or not used the assessment information. Quality use of pre- and ongoing assessment requires informed work, persistent reflection about that work, and the willingness to keep at it. It's a bit like exercise. Going to the gym once or twice doesn't accomplish much.

Critical as it is in supporting student success, however, assessment to inform instruction is not a stand-alone element in an effectively differentiated classroom. Effective use of formative assessment is impossible without clearly articulated, engaging, and complex learning goals (KUDs), or without tight alignment between an assessment and the KUDs it's intended to assess. In other words, without robust curriculum, formative assessment is likely to be insipid, ill focused, or both. Again, the common sense is evident. The power of assessment to inform teaching and learning derives from the power of curriculum to engage learners and guide them in understanding and acting upon ideas that are pivotal in the disciplines. And again, the work required to ensure quality curriculum is demanding and ongoing.

Effective instruction is dependent on both formative assessment and curriculum. It is shaped by curriculum. Flat, one-dimensional curriculum yields flat, one-dimensional instruction. Effective instruction is also responsive to learners as individuals rather than as a "flock." Therefore, effective instruction is necessarily informed by persistent assessment *for* and *as* instruction in order to provide the teacher with evolving images of the evolving learning trajectories of the diverse students in a classroom. Assessment *for* and *as* instruction is a potent catalyst for differentiation. It's almost impossible to study the results of such assessments and not see the reality that students came away from a lesson or series of lessons in very different places—no matter how convinced we are that our teaching was brilliant. At that point, differentiation isn't an "extra" that we might consider if there were additional time. Rather, differentiation is simply the next logical, common-sense step in teaching (Earl, 2003). Instructional planning is, or ought to be, entwined with curriculum and assessment in that assessment contents are dictated by curricular specificity about what constitutes essential knowledge, which specific skills must be a focus of learning, and which understandings act as a "magnetic field" for the knowledge and skills. In turn, assessment results will reveal student status with each of those elements. Finally, those results should inform a teacher's choice of instructional strategies as well as teaching and learning sequences. Some students will have mastered essential vocabulary, for instance, when others still struggle with unfamiliar words. Some students will compare and contrast, or defend a position, or design a test for a hypothesis quite competently, while others are at the front door of developing those skills. Some students will provide thoughtful illustrations of the understanding that "Math is a language to describe the world around us," while others are only able to

Figure 7.1
A Summary of Assessment Throughout an Instructional Cycle

	Pre-assessment	Ongoing Assessment	Summative Assessment	Student Self-assessment
Why	• To determine students' status relative to targeted KUDs, as well as interests and learning preferences as a unit begins	• To monitor students' learning needs relative to targeted KUDs, as well as to monitor interests and approaches to learning that may or may not be working well	• To determine the level of mastery each student has obtained with the targeted KUDs at key junctures in a unit	• To help students connect effort and growth • To engage each student in thinking about his or her own learning progress and needs • To help students develop strategies that support their learning
How	• Use a range of methods in a variety of formats (formal and informal) that make visible students' current standing relative to targeted KUDs	• Use a range of methods in a variety of formats (formal and informal) that make visible students' current standing relative to targeted KUDs	• Use a range of methods in a variety of formats (closed and performance) that assess both process and product outcomes	• Elicit student metacognition and reflection on performance at critical points in a unit of study

	Pre-assessment	Ongoing Assessment	Summative Assessment	Student Self-assessment
Quality	• Clearly defined learning outcomes (KUDs) • Tight alignment with the KUDs	• Clearly defined learning outcomes (KUDs) • Descriptive and detailed feedback to each student (if using formal methods)	• Accuracy, consistency, and fairness based on high-quality information • Clearly identified learning targets (KUDs) • Accurate reporting	• Students engaged in self-reflection, including monitoring and adjusting process • Students challenging their own learning
Use	• Provides information to guide differentiation of instruction as a unit of study begins	• Provides each student with accurate descriptive feedback • Provides information that can inform conversations between teacher and students • Yields information to guide planning for differentiated instruction • Provides descriptive information to stakeholders (teachers, parents) about student learning	• Indicates each student's standing relative to the targeted KUDs at critical points in a learning cycle • Provides a basis for grading	• Allows students to focus on the process of learning rather than simply right or wrong answers • Provides information for conversations between teacher and students • Can support independent student learning

provide concrete and evident illustrations, or no illustrations at all. Those realities provide the teacher's marching orders for instructional decision making.

Those realities also bind classroom leadership and management to curriculum, assessment, and instruction. On some days it will be necessary for the teacher to meet with a small group of students to preteach academic vocabulary, extend the challenge level of a writing assignment, or reteach a skill that some students didn't grasp the day before. On some days it will be necessary for students to work with a tiered task or wise for them to have the option of working alone or in pairs or triads. On some days it will make a positive difference in learning if students can use a variety of print or digital resources or if they can study models of quality student work done at various levels of complexity. In all these instances and a legion of other possibilities, flexible classroom routines are mandatory. Thus to accomplish what needs to be done to move each learner forward, the teacher has two roles in regard to classroom management. One is to develop routines and processes that allow more than one thing at a time to take place in the classroom—and to take place efficiently and effectively. The second is to enlist the understanding and partnership of students in creating a classroom that works for everyone. The common sense here is that if we have evidence that kids differ as learners—and we do—then classrooms that require everyone to work in rigid ways simply will fail many students. And so classroom management for differentiation asks the teacher to become an orchestra conductor—aware of and immersed in a common score, but at the same time attentive to the role and dynamics of various sections of the orchestra, and providing guidance and structure to ensure that each section functions as it should in order to contribute to a successful performance of the whole. Simply put, managing a differentiated classroom calls on a teacher to be a leader—not a dictator or a drill sergeant. It calls on the teacher to create a team or community around the shared goal of successful learning and to teach students the skills and processes necessary to contribute appropriately to that team.

The final element of effectively differentiated classrooms is learning environment, which is in many ways the most potent of the elements. Real learning requires struggle, and that particular struggle somehow lays us bare as we contemplate what might lie ahead: *Perhaps I'll fail. Perhaps I'll look foolish or incompetent or incapable. Perhaps I can't live up to this most defining of human traits—making sense of and having dominion over the world around me. Maybe peers will make fun of me. Maybe the teacher—a powerful person in the life of a learner at any age—will think poorly of me or expect more than I can give.* Creating a classroom environment that invites every student to learn and that fuels the learning process also calls on teachers to be leaders. But in this instance, the leader is one who balances challenge and support, who dignifies both the learner and the learning, who understands the fragility of being young and vulnerable and who therefore offers a harbor for learning. Van Manen (1991) expresses it well:

Leading means going first, and in going first, you can trust me, for I have tested the ice. I have lived. I now know something of the rewards as well as the trappings of growing toward adulthood and making a world for yourself. Although the going first is no guarantee of success (because the world is not without risks and dangers), in the pedagogical relationship, there is a more fundamental guarantee: No matter what, I am here. And you can count on me. (p. 38)

When a teacher not only earns the trust of students but also teaches them to be trustworthy with one another, nearly anything is possible, and everything in the classroom is designed to make that belief more than make-believe.

For many teachers, planning for, thinking about, or even accepting the primacy of the five key elements of differentiation—and of powerful teaching—seems like too much. And yet, the novice teacher who spoke of the common sense of the elements makes a compelling argument for their logic. So perhaps as with all worthwhile and therefore necessarily complex ideas, what matters most is beginning to live with the idea, to try it out, and to learn from experience.

This book argues that thoughtful implementation of assessment *for* and *as* instruction is a fine place to begin with differentiation. Lorna Earl (2003) reminds us that "finding out about students as learners and people is the key to differentiation" (p. 87). She explains that differentiation doesn't mean a different set of lesson plans for every student, nor does it mean using ability grouping to reduce the student differences a teacher must think about. Rather, she says, it means recognizing and accepting the reality that students are unique individuals and using what we can learn about each student to plan instruction that optimizes learning for every one of them. "When teachers are equipped with detailed knowledge about their students and have a clear idea about what the students need to learn, differentiation can happen all the time" (p. 87). We agree. And we invite you to hone your practice of informed assessment to inform teaching and learning.

Appendix: Suggested Readings in Differentiated Instruction

The following books can further your understanding of differentiated instruction in general and of the role of learning environment, curriculum, instruction, and classroom leadership and management in a differentiated classroom.

Differentiated Instruction in General

Sousa, D., & Tomlinson, C. A. (2011). *Differentiation and the brain: How neuroscience supports the learner-friendly classroom.* Bloomington, IN: Solution Tree.

Tomlinson, C. A. (2001). *How to differentiate instruction in mixed-ability classrooms* (2nd ed.). Alexandria, VA: ASCD.

Learning Environment in a Differentiated Classroom

Tomlinson, C. A. (2004). *Fulfilling the promise of the differentiated classroom: Strategies and tools for responsive teaching.* Alexandria, VA: ASCD.

Curriculum in a Differentiated Classroom

Tomlinson, C. A., & McTighe, J. (2006). *Integrating differentiated instruction and Understanding by Design: Connecting content and kids.* Alexandria, VA: ASCD.

Instruction in a Differentiated Classroom

Tomlinson, C. A. (1999). *The differentiated classroom: Responding to the needs of all learners.* Alexandria, VA: ASCD.

Classroom Leadership and Management in a Differentiated Classroom

Tomlinson, C. A., & Imbeau, M. (2010). *Leading and managing a differentiated classroom.* Alexandria, VA: ASCD.

References

Airasian, P. (1997). *Classroom assessment* (3rd ed.). New York: McGraw-Hill.

Allen, J., Gregory, A., Mikami, J., Hamre, B., & Pianta, R. (2012). *Predicting adolescent achievement with the CLASS-S observation tool*. A CASTL Research Brief. Charlottesville, VA: University of Virginia, Curry School of Education.

Asimov, I. (1950). *I, robot*. New York: Bantam Dell.

Ausubel, D. (1968). *Educational psychology: A cognitive view*. New York: Holt, Rinehart, &Winston.

Berger, R. (2003). *An ethic of excellence: Building a culture of craftsmanship with students*. Portsmouth, NH: Heinemann.

Black, P., & Wiliam, D. (1998). Inside the black box: Raising standards through formative assessment. *Phi Delta Kappan, 80*, 139–144, 146–148.

Black, P., & Wiliam, D. (2009). Developing the theory of formative assessment. *Educational Assessment, Evaluation, and Accountability, 21*(1), 5–31.

Brookhart, S. (2004). *Grading*. Upper Saddle River, NJ: Merrill/Prentice Hall.

Brookhart, S. (2012). Preventing feedback fizzle. *Educational Leadership, 70*(1), 25–29.

Brookhart, S. (2013). Grading. In J. H. McMillan (Ed.), *SAGE handbook of research on classroom assessment* (pp. 257–272). Los Angeles: SAGE.

Brown, A. (1994). The advancement of learning. *Educational Researcher, 23*, 4–12.

Chappius, J. (2012). How am I doing? *Educational Leadership, 70*(1), 36–41.

Chappius, J., Stiggins, R., Chappius, S., & Arter, J. (2012). *Assessment for learning: Doing it right, using it well* (2nd ed.). Upper Saddle River, NJ: Pearson.

Clements, A. (2004). *The report card*. New York: Simon & Schuster.

Coffield, F., Moseley, D., Hall, E., & Ecclestone, K. (2004). *Should we be using learning styles? What research has to say to practice*. London: Learning and Skills Research Centre.

Costa, A., & Kallick, B. (2008). *Learning and leading with habits of mind: 16 essential characteristics for success*. Alexandria, VA: ASCD.

Courey, A., Balogh, J., Siker, J., & Paik, J. (2012). Academic music: Music instruction to engage third-grade students in learning basic fraction concepts. *Educational Studies in Mathematics*. DOI 10.1007/510649-012-9395-9.

Dressel, P. (1983). Grades: One more tilt at the windmill. In A. Chickering (Ed.), *Bulletin*. Memphis: Memphis State University, Center for the Study of Higher Education.

Dweck, C. (2008). *Mindset: The new psychology of success*. New York: Ballantine.

Earl, L. (2003). *Assessment as learning: Using classroom assessment to maximize student learning*. Thousand Oaks, CA: Corwin.

Eliot, L. (2009). *Pink brain, blue brain: How small differences grow into troublesome gaps and what we can do about it.* New York: Houghton Mifflin Harcourt.

Ginott, H. (1972). *Teacher and child: A book for parents and teachers.* New York: Macmillan.

Gurian, M. (2001). *Boys and girls learn differently: A guide for teachers and parents.* San Francisco: Jossey-Bass.

Guskey, T. (1996). *Communicating student learning: The ASCD yearbook, 1996.* Alexandria, VA: ASCD.

Guskey, T. (2006). Making high school grades meaningful. *Phi Delta Kappan, 87,* 670–675.

Hansberry, L. (1958). *A raisin in the sun.* New York: Random House.

Hattie, J. (2009). *Visible learning: A synthesis of over 800 meta-analyses relating to achievement.* New York: Routledge.

Hattie, J. (2012a). Know thy impact. *Educational Leadership, 70*(1), 18–23.

Hattie, J. (2012b). *Visible learning for teachers: Maximizing impact on learning.* New York: Routledge.

Hess, K. (2010, December). *Learning progressions frameworks designed for the Common Core State Standards in Mathematics, K–12.* Dover, NH: National Center for the Improvement of Educational Assessment (NCIEA).

Hess, K. (2011, December). *Learning progressions frameworks designed for use with the Common Core State Standards in English Language Arts & Literacy K–12.* Dover, NH: National Center for the Improvement of Educational Assessment (NCIEA).

LePage, P., Darling-Hammond, L., & Akar, H. (2005). Classroom management. In L. Darling-Hammond & J. Bransford (Eds.), *Preparing teachers for a changing world: What teachers should learn and be able to do* (pp. 327–357). San Francisco: Jossey-Bass.

Lisle, A. M. (2006). *Cognitive neuroscience in education: Mapping neuro-cognitive processes and structures to learning styles, can it be done?* Retrieved from http://www.leeds.ac.uk/educol/documents/157290.htm.

Marzano, R. (2010). *Formative assessment and standards-based grading.* Bloomington, IN: Marzano Research Laboratory.

Moon, T., Callahan, C., Brighton, C., & Tomlinson, C. A. (2002). *Development of differentiated performance tasks for middle school classrooms.* (RM 02160). Storrs, CT: University of Connecticut, NRC/GT.

National Research Council. (2000). *How people learn: Brain, mind, experience, and school.* Washington, DC: National Academy Press.

National Research Council. (2001). *Knowing what students know: The science and design of educational assessment.* Washington, DC: National Academy Press.

O'Connor, K. (2011). *A repair kit for grading: 15 fixes for broken grades* (2nd ed.). Boston: Pearson.

Pashler, H., McDaniel, M., Rohrer, D., & Bjork, R. (2008). Learning styles: Concepts and evidence. *Psychological Science in the Public Interest, 9*(3), 106–119.

Perricone, J. (2005). *Zen and the art of public school teaching.* Frederick, MD: Publish America.

Popham, J. (2007). The lowdown on learning progressions. *Educational Leadership, 64*(7), 83–84.

Salomone, R. (2003). *Same, different, equal: Re-thinking single-sex schooling.* New Haven, CT: Yale University Press.

Schlechty, P. (1997). *Inventing better schools: An action plan for educational reform.* San Francisco: Jossey-Bass.

Skinner, E., Furrer, C., Marchand, G., & Kindermann, T. (2008). Engagement and disaffection in the classroom: Part of a larger motivational dynamic? *Journal of Educational Psychology, 100,* 765–781.

Sousa, D. A., & Tomlinson, C. A. (2011). *Differentiation and the brain: How neuroscience supports the learner-friendly classroom.* Bloomington, IN: Solution Tree Press.

Sparks, S. (2012, September 26). Studies probe power of "personalizing" algebra. *Education Week*. Retrieved from http://edweek.org/ew/articles/2012/09/26/05personalize_ep.h32.html?print=1

State Collaborative on Assessment and Student Standards. (2008). *Attributes of effective formative assessment*. Washington, DC: Council of Chief State School Officers.

Sternberg, R., Torff, B., & Grigorenko, E. (1998). Teaching triarchically improves student achievement. *Journal of Educational Psychology, 90*, 374–384.

Stiggins, R. (2001). *Student-involved classroom assessment* (3rd ed.). Upper Saddle River, NJ: Pearson.

Stiggins, R. (2006). Making high school grades meaningful. *Phi Delta Kappan, 87*, 670–675.

Storti, C. (1999). *Figuring foreigners out: A practical guide.* Yarmouth, ME: Intercultural Press.

Tannen, D. (1990). *You just don't understand: Men and women in conversation.* New York: Ballantine.

Tomlinson, C. A. (2003). *Fulfilling the promise of the differentiated classroom: Strategies and tools for responsive teaching*. Alexandria, VA: ASCD.

Tomlinson, C. A., & Imbeau, M. (2013). Differentiated instruction: An integration of theory and practice. In B. Irby, G. Brown, R. Lara-Aiecio, & S. Jackson (Eds.), *Handbook of educational theories* (pp. 1081–1101). Charlotte, NC: Information Age Publishing.

Tomlinson, C. A., & McTighe, J. (2006). *Integrating differentiated instruction and Understanding by Design: Connecting content and kids*. Alexandria, VA: ASCD.

Tomlinson, C. A., & Moon, T. (2013). Differentiation and classroom assessment. In J. H. McMillan (Ed.), *SAGE handbook of research on classroom assessment* (pp. 415–430). Los Angeles: SAGE.

Trumbull, E., Rothstein-Fish, C., Greenfield, P., & Quiroz, B. (2001). *Bridging cultures between home and school: A quick guide for teachers.* Mahwah, NJ: Lawrence Erlbaum.

Van Manen, M. (1991). *The tact of teaching: Toward a pedagogy of thoughtfulness*. Albany, NY: State University of New York.

Vygotsky, L. S. (1978). *Mind in society: The development of higher psychological processes*. Cambridge, MA: Harvard University Press.

Wiggins, G. (1993). *Assessing student performance*. San Francisco: Jossey-Bass.

Wiggins, G. (1998). Educative assessment : Designing assessments to inform and improve student performance. San Francisco, CA: Jossey-Bass

Wiggins, G., & McTighe, J. (2008, May). Put understanding first. *Educational Leadership, 65*(8), 36–41.

Wiggins, G. (2012). 7 keys to effective feedback. *Educational Leadership, 70*(1), 11–16.

Wiggins, G., & McTighe, J. (1998). *Understanding by Design*. Alexandria, VA: ASCD.

Wiliam, D. (2011). *Embedded formative assessment*. Indianapolis, IN: Solution Tree.

Wiliam, D. (2012). Feedback: Part of a system. *Educational Leadership, 70*(1), 31–34.

Willis, J. (2006). *Research-based strategies to ignite student learning: Insights from a neurologist and classroom teacher*. Alexandria, VA: ASCD.

Willis, J. (2007). *Brain-friendly strategies for the inclusion classroom*. Alexandria, VA: ASCD.

Yeh, S. (2011). *The cost-effectiveness of 22 approaches for raising student achievement*. Charlotte, NC: Information Age.

Index

The letter *f* following a page number denotes a figure.

About the Authors

Carol Ann Tomlinson was a classroom teacher for 21 years, working with high school, pre-school, and middle school students, as well as administering district programs for struggling and advanced learners. She was named Virginia's Teacher of the Year in 1974. She is currently on the faculty at the University of Virginia where she is William Clay Parrish, Jr., Professor, Chair of Educational Leadership, Foundations, and Policy, and Co-Director of the University's Institutes on Academic Diversity. Carol was named Outstanding Professor at UVa's Curry School of Education in 2004 and received an All-University Teaching Award in 2008. Her books on differentiated instruction are available in 13 languages. She works with teachers in the United States and internationally to develop classrooms that provide effective instruction for academically diverse student populations.

Tonya R. Moon is a Professor in the Curry School of Education at the University of Virginia. Her specializations are in the areas of educational measurement, research, and evaluation, and she works with educational institutions nationally and internationally on issues associated with educational assessments. She also works with school districts and schools on using better assessment techniques for improving instruction and student learning. In addition to her research and teaching responsibilities, she is the Chair of the university's Institutional Review Board for the Social and Behavioral Sciences.

Related ASCD Resources: Differentiated Instruction

At the time of publication, the following ASCD resources were available; for the most up-to-date information about ASCD resources, go to www.ascd.org. ASCD stock numbers are noted in parentheses.

DVDs

Leadership for Differentiating Instruction (one 100-minute DVD with a comprehensive user guide and bonus DVD features) (#607038)

A Visit to a School Moving Toward Differentiation (one 30-minute DVD with a comprehensive viewer's guide) (#607133)

Mixed Media

Differentiating Instruction for Mixed-Ability Classrooms Professional Inquiry Kit by Carol Ann Tomlinson (#196213)

Differentiated Instruction Professional Development Planner and Resource Package (Stage 1) (#701225)

Differentiated Instruction Professional Development Planner and Resource Package (Stage 2) (#703402)

Online Courses

Differentiated Instruction: Creating an Environment That Supports Learning (#PD11OC118)

Differentiated Instruction: Using Assessment Effectively (#PD09OC12)

Differentiated Instruction: Using Ongoing Assessment to Inform Instruction (#PD11OC117)

Print Products

The Differentiated Classroom: Responding to the Needs of All Learners by Carol Ann Tomlinson (#199040)

The Differentiated School: Making Revolutionary Changes in Teaching and Learning by Carol Ann Tomlinson, Lane Narvaez, and Kay Brimijoin (#105005)

Fulfilling the Promise of the Differentiated Classroom: Strategies and Tools for Responsive Teaching by Carol Ann Tomlinson (#103107)

How to Differentiate Instruction in Mixed-Ability Classrooms, 2nd Edition by Carol Ann Tomlinson (#101043)

Integrating Differentiated Instruction and Understanding by Design: Connecting Content and Kids by Carol Ann Tomlinson and Jay McTighe (#105004)

THE WHOLE CHILD The Whole Child Initiative helps schools and communities create learning environments that allow students to be healthy, safe, engaged, supported, and challenged. To learn more about other books and resources that relate to the whole child, visit www.wholechildeducation.org.

For additional resources, visit us on the World Wide Web (http://www.ascd.org), send an e-mail message to member@ascd.org, call the ASCD Service Center (1-800-933-ASCD or 703-578-9600, then press 2), send a fax to 703-575-5400, or write to Information Services, ASCD, 1703 N. Beauregard St., Alexandria, VA 22311-1714 USA.